DESPICABLE
SPECIES

Other Books by Janet Lembke:

River Time
Looking for Eagles
Dangerous Birds
Skinny Dipping
Shake Them 'Simmons Down

DESPICABLE SPECIES

On Cowbirds, Kudzu, Hornworms, and Other Scourges

Janet Lembke

Illustrations by Joe Nutt

The Lyons Press

10 9 8 7 6 5 4 3 2 1

FIRST EDITION

Library of Congress Cataloging-in-Publication Data

Lembke, Janet.
    Despicable species : cowbirds, kudzu, and other scourges / Janet
Lembke : illustrations by Joe Nutt.
       p.   cm.
    Includes bibliographical references (p.   ).
    ISBN 1-55821-635-9
   ⌊1. Symbiosis.   2. Parasitism.   I. Title.
QH548.L46   1999
577.8'5—dc21   99-15220
                                                         CIP

Permission from the following to quote copyrighted material is gratefully acknowledged:

    Alfred A. Knopf: eighteen-line excerpt from "The Great Scarf of Birds" from *Collected Poems,
1953–1993* by John Updike. Copyright © 1995 by John Updike.

    HarperCollins Publishers, Inc.: four-line excerpt from "Mushrooms" from *The Collected Poems*
by Sylvia Plath. Copyright © 1981 by Ted Hughes.

    University Press of New England: eleven-line excerpt from "Kudzu" from *Helmets* by James
Dickey. Copyright © 1962, 1963, 1964 by James Dickey.

    Viking Penguin: six-line excerpt from *The Odyssey* translated by Robert Fagles. Copyright
© Robert Fagles, 1996.

Several pieces have appeared in somewhat different form in these publications:

    "The Natural History of Proteus," "Unfinished Business," "Heritage," "Prospect and
Refuge," "A Foot in the Door," *Brightleaf: A Southern Review of Books*, Vol. 1, Nos. 1–4;
Vol 2, No. 2.

    "The Riddles of the Sphinx," *Oxford American*, Issue No. 29.

    "Murmurations," *Bird Watcher's Digest*, Vol. 20, No. 4.

For three people
who are all at the farthest remove from despicability:
Harriet Divoky
Jean Wilson Kraus
JoAnne Powell

CONTENTS

ACKNOWLEDGMENTS

As always, many people have contributed information and recounted, with the proper glee and shudders, anecdotes of their own encounters with despicable species. Some of these good people are fully named in the stories. Others who deserve a share of credit are listed below:

- Bob Marlin; Nick Lyons; Southern writers Franklin Burroughs, James Kilgo, John Lane, Janisse Ray, "Prospect and Refuge"
- Franklin Burroughs, Ruth Roberson, "The Barkings of a Joyful Squirrel"
- Grace Evans, Meg Rawls, "The Natural History of Proteus"
- Jeffery Beam; Bob Marlin; Michael Waldvogel, North Carolina Cooperative Extension Service, "Legs"
- Nick Lyons, "Blood" and "Unfinished Business"
- Tom Glasgow, cooperative extension agent, New Bern, North Carolina; F. Timothy Edwards, landscape architect, South Carolina Department of Transportation, "Heritage"
- Sara Mack, "The Wisdom of Nature"
- Staff and patrons of the Augusta County Library, Fishersville, Virginia, questionnaire
- Field-trippers who came to Great Neck Point under the auspices of the North Carolina Maritime Museum, questionnaire
- Liz Lathrop and the Oriental Birders, questionnaire

Nor should my entertaining husband, the Chief, and my supportive friends, especially Nick and my editor Lilly Golden at the Lyons Press, be ignored. To all of you and to any whom I may have overlooked, my deepest thanks. From now on, may you remain unbitten, unblistered, and unstung.

The real, which is perfectly simple and supremely beautiful, too often escapes us, giving way before the imaginary, which is less troublesome to acquire. Instead of going back to the facts and seeing for ourselves, we blindly follow tradition.

—Jean Henri Fabre

DESPICABLE
SPECIES

LIVING TOGETHER, LIKE IT OR NOT

American Dog Tick (*Dermacentor variabilis*)

An Introduction

HOW do we deal with the bad stuff? With all those disgusting, sickening, despicable, repellently alien lives that impinge on ours?

The world offers much to cherish and admire. Roses, oak trees, butterflies, ladybugs, bald eagles, dolphins, and puppies—these are among the thousand thousand things, great and small, that delight both spirit and imagination. They lend their fragrances to our lives, shade our summer days, bring fluttering color to the flowers, eat the pests that eat our gardens, soar to give us models for our aspirations, leap and roll with glistening power in sight and in mind's eye, and lick us, love us unconditionally. The subjects of our fondness are—only the mean-hearted would dispute it—Good with a capital G.

Other lives connect with ours in less all-out friendly ways. Some are neutral, asking only—if they ask at all—for the kind of attention that is easily given: a deer browsing at wood's edge, a red-tailed hawk perched in a roadside tree, swamp roses sprouting in a drainage ditch, June bugs thudding on doors and window screens. And there are lives so minuscule that we absolutely fail to notice them, like the pillow mites that subsist on the bits of skin we slough off as we sleep. Still other lives affect ours in ways that require work, as when oregano assumes its takeover mode in the herb garden or the neighbors' cats dance, leaving footprints all over the car. Then we weed or we wash. But the plants and animals causing events like these fall into the acceptable range—except when the puppy eats one of a pair of new shoes or the browsing deer is suddenly impelled to bound into the path of an oncoming car.

And then there are the lives that people love to hate: aggressive weeds, slithering or pulsating creatures that trigger the shudder factor, and the bugs, oh, the bugs in their teeming millions that ruin summer nights, crunch unpleasantly underfoot, deliver painful stings, or draw blood with their stabbing, sucking mouths. Sometimes, as with scraps of life so small we cannot see them—bacteria, viruses, dinoflagellates—they sicken and they kill.

Yet we're stuck on this earth together. And one small word

describes the immense and unimaginable array of alliances, conspiracies, collisions, and entanglements that mark our lives: *symbiosis*. It simply means "living together" but encompasses the not-so-simple fact that every plant and animal, and every other squirming, blooming, often invisible form of life, conducts its affairs, want to or not, in some kind of relationship with neighbors quite unlike itself.

In grade school, I thought that symbiosis was invariably a good thing, an always friendly conjoining of vital forces to achieve a common good. Back then, the lowly lichens were my introduction to the concept. I've since come to appreciate how quirky they are: gray-green, yellow, or reddish brown, leafy or crusty, they grow on trees, grow on rocks, and thrive equally well in heat or cold. And how oddly useful, for they not only serve as the food of choice to reindeer and caribou but also provide surprisingly flamboyant colors, purple and glowing rose-red, to the dyer's trade. And how utterly improbable! A fungus and an alga, the latter sometimes of the blue-green sort but often the green *Protococcus*, mingle in an inseparable union. More than that, the union amalgamates two distinct biological kingdoms, that of the Fungi and that of the Monera. The Monera, as immemorially ancient as the advent of life on earth, comprises one-celled organisms, like bacteria, that lack a nucleus, and, indeed, cyanobacteria—blue bacteria—is another name for blue-green algae. Each of a lichen's components helps the other, alga by producing vitamins, fungus by absorbing necessary water from the air, both by exchanging the discrete carbohydrates that each manufactures. Neither can exist alone. The situation is win-win all around.

But turn the natural world's kaleidoscope and look elsewhere: it's clear that relationships come in a hodgepodge of forms, some grand, some grotesque, with every possible permutation in between. Sometimes the relationships—and resemblances—are close indeed. Take, for example, the seven species of woodpecker that I observe in both my homes, the Shenandoah Valley and coastal North Carolina. Sometimes two species work for food—*tock-ta-tock-tock*—on the same tree. The food-gathering relationships here include the social mix of bird and bird, the birds' bark-chiseling or sap-seeking behavior on the tree, and the birds' predation on the insect cafeteria caught in the sap or hidden beneath the bark. More often, however, physically disparate actors are intertwined in a boggling array of situations and positions. Fungal threads snuggle by harmonious necessity with the roots of trees; behold, a crop of morel mushrooms at the base of a sweet gum. A ghost-pale isopod makes itself at home first as parasite, then as tenant in the menhaden's mouth; the fish suffers little while the hanger-on thrives. The HIV virus must live and replicate in the human body; as it does so, it entombs itself. All of these relationships are symbiotic, but win-win is hardly the rule. Instead, the business of living together throws friends, enemies, and bystanders onto the same patch of earth. Some get along famously or find neutral ground. Others, to ensure the replication of their kind, succeed in fighting to the death.

Science identifies several distinct styles of symbiosis. It is Burwell Wingfield, teacher of biology at Virginia Military Institute and expert hunter of morels, who names and explains these associations to me, and diagrams them with a symbol—Plus, Minus, or Zero—to indicate benefit, harm, or a neutral outcome for each for the two parties involved.

The first style is mutualism, a top-of-the-line Plus-Plus. It describes the kind of partnership in which two unrelated species work together, each supporting the other, because the lives of both depend upon the association. This is the lichens' win-win style, and that of the yucca plants and their specially adapted moths: plant needs moth for pollination, moth needs plant for larval food. And the relationship is obligate—it must occur, that is, in order for either partner to survive.

The second is protocooperation, the other Plus-Plus arrangement. The word was coined by Warder Clyde Allee (1885–1955), an ecologist with a particular interest in the communities of marine life-forms, and it refers to a rudimentary, always involuntary sort of teamwork. The association is passive; a common good is achieved without awareness or intent on the part of any symbiont. Mixed schools of fish, mixed flocks of birds engage in this behavior; when one species finds food or encounters a threat, the other species in the aggregation are alerted. Another protocooperative effort occurs between a tree and the sow bugs, centipedes, and other small creatures that live in the larder of leaf mold provided by the tree; as they feed, they churn and aerate the soil, helping the tree capture the moisture and nutrients necessary to its growth. Protocooperation also takes on darker guises. One that sorely afflicts people is the opportunistic association of the *Borrelia* spirochete (a relative of syphilis) with *Fusobacterium,* one of its Moneran kin; when the two occur on the same human gum at the same time, their joined forces cause the galloping form of gingivitis known as trench mouth. (If the sufferer is included in this symbiotic equation, then we're looking at parasitism, but more of that shortly).

Commensalism—which comes from Latin words that mean "together at the same table"—rates Plus-Zero in the symbiosis stakes. One party, usually the smaller, gains, while its larger host is unaffected. This is the relationship that occurs between the menhaden and its isopod (its "nursemaid" in folk parlance); after the juvenile isopod, lodged in the menhaden's gills, matures, it abandons its parasitic ways to become a boarder in the menhaden's mouth, where it helps itself liberally to the plankton soup swept in by its host. Commensalism is also the mode de vivre between our kind and the starling when the bird probes for insect food beneath the earth of a manmade clearing. And it's the kind of association seen in barnyard or pasture where cowbirds and cattle egrets tag along behind cows and horses to batten on the bugs that the larger animals have stirred up in passing.

A fourth style of symbiosis, the Plus-Minus version, takes two forms: parasistism and predation. Parasitism is by far the most common form of symbiosis on this earth. Always, one party gains, while the other forfeits resources and sometimes its life. Sometimes parasitism is obligate, sometimes opportunistic, as when a species takes temporary advantage of another's nest or cache of food. A parasite's host may be restricted to one particular organism (potato for the fungal potato blight, human being for the bacterial trench mouth). A two-host arrangement may also occur, in which the parasite, halfway through its life cycle, moves from one bed-and-breakfast to another (such as pig, then human being for the pork tapeworm). Or the possible hosts may be many, a diverse group of equally succulent and nutritive possibilities: any passing warm-blooded animal, like dog, deer, or person, is capable of satisfying an American dog tick's craving for protein. The parasites may even pile up in a scenario called hyperparasitism; the dog tick, for example, that sups on mammalian blood may itself be host to two kinds of internal microscopic organisms, each of which depends for its very life on tick juice. This arrangement demonstrates the fact that there are ectoparasites and endoparasites—those like the tick that work from the outside and those that work only on inside jobs. In every case, the host is larger than the invader and also serves as its only source of food.

Another kind of parasitism does not involve one creature munching directly on another but is rather a mooching arrangement—social parasitism. It occurs in a stunning array of variations, notably among the ants (though it comes in a human version, too: the legend of the man who came for dinner but stayed on for years). In every variant, one species associates itself intimately with another and gains benefits like food and shelter from the association. Two of the many apparitions of this phenomenon are cleptobiosis ("life-stealing"), in which one species lives near or among another and either feeds upon the host colony's refuse or robs its workers, and dulosis ("slavery"), a symbiosis noted by Darwin in *On the Origin of Species*, in which one kind of ant takes the workers of another kind captive and sets them to such necessary tasks as food storage, nest building, and caring for the slave-maker's brood. Ants and wasps also engage in an extreme form of social parasitism called inquilinism, from the Latin *inquilinus*, meaning "someone who inhabits a place not his own." In the case of insects, the mooching species moves into its host's nest; there, coercing the host to deliver vital services, it degenerates physically, becoming unable to care for itself in any matters other than reproduction.

As for the predatory form of the Plus-Minus symbiosis, the seeker of prey behaves in much the way as a parasite, though it certainly puts more muscle and greater agility into its work, sometimes hunting down its food and sometimes, like the angler fish and various spiders, enticing it. And the predator has greater choices than the parasite when it comes to taking advantage of whatever nutritious opportunity comes galloping, swimming, or creeping into range. Nor is the predator always larger than its prey (think of a lion bringing down a zebra, or a man shooting a deer).

Curiously, both parasite and predator may enhance the well-being of the prey species. For the sake of future meals, the former does not kill a healthy host. The latter tends to kill and eat the weakest individuals. Plus-Minus symbioses may seem repellent to us—the stab-and-grab attentions of lions or mosquitoes, the stealthy single-mindedness of a cat waiting to pounce, the cowbird and red-head duck dumping their eggs in another species' nest, the pestilential viruses afflicting throats and sinuses with the common cold—but in the long run they actually work to strengthen prey species and help them adapt to life in an unforgiving world. As Burwell Wingfield says, "The parasites and predators are merely trying to survive. In order for them (or us) to live, something must die, be it plant or animal. It is the nature of life."

The business of living together includes one Zero-Minus combination, in which one party profits not at all but the other invariably loses. It's known as amensalism—"being shoved away from the table"—and it takes two forms, competition and antibiosis. In both forms, resources—food, water, and space—are at stake. The bigger, stronger species helps itself, while the smaller, weaker species goes without, declining or altogether dying out. The competitive form of amensalism puts on a vigorous green show in our North Carolina vegetable garden every year. For every pea and bean seed planted, a hydra-headed batch of weeds springs up—jimson, bindweed, nut grass, witchgrass, rabbit tobacco, cranesbill, and several dozen others, all jostling and pushing. The harvest would fail except that I also move into a competitive mode, wielding rake and hoe. Antibiosis is less visible and more insidious. It is nothing less than chemical warfare, with the unaffected species secreting toxins that inhibit or kill the other party or parties within its reach. Think of antibiotics like penicillin, a bread-mold secretion, and the nitrogenous compound allantoin, excreted by maggots; both kill bacteria (and in so doing, add considerably to human comfort). The black walnut tree also engages in such tactics, secreting juglone, a substance that poisons plants trying to grow within its root zone. There is no profit in this gambit, except that, at the very beginning, when the sprouted black walnut seed puts down its first roots, it discourages competition; once established, however, the tree needs no toxin to maintain its dominance. Not long after moving into our Virginia house, we cut down the black walnut, a squirrel-planted volunteer, that had seized dominion over the small back yard. The ground beneath was bare of grass, not to mention weeds. It took five years, and the deaths of two live Christmas trees, before the juglone had dissipated enough for new greenery to take hold in the poisoned soil. Behaving at times like black walnut trees, people also practice antibiosis by spreading herbicides in the hope of a perfectly weed-free lawn (though what perfection there might be in weedlessness, I do not see).

The final incarnation of symbiosis, the bleak Minus-Minus version, is synnecrosis—a Greek term that means "dying together." In a situation akin to that of the feuding Hatfields and McCoys, mutual inhibition occurs between two species. And both may die because of the fast-as-a-bullet toxins released into the shared habitat. Burwell Wingfield illustrates this lose-lose arrangement with a general example from the strange and populous kingdom of the fungi: "Suppose the genus *Penicillium* contains a species X, which produces a particularly strong variation of the antibiotic penicillin. This might be toxic to a species of the genus *Streptomyces*. Suppose also that species *Y* of the genus *Streptomyces* produces a variation of streptomycin that is toxic to *Penicillium X*. If these two fungi growing in the soil encounter each other, both will react to the antibiotics, and that part of both fungal filaments in the vicinity will be killed." But, where win-lose scenarios may occur on both an individual and a species basis, lose-lose synnecrosis spells doom only for individuals. It does not portend the end of any species. The species have evolved their own survival strategies, have devised blind, unstoppable means of perpetuating themselves. Wingfield notes that synnecrosis takes place mainly between organisms living in the soil, but he speculates with a wry shake of his head that, given the ongoing savagery in places like Bosnia, Kosovo, Kurdistan, Rwanda, Somalia, and Ireland, it has spilled over onto mankind.

So here we are, every last one of us, living together, like it or not. As for the lives large and small that we don't like living with, what is it about them (or us) that drives us to profanity, lifts our swatting hands, or excites our shudders? Peculiarly, out of the whole breathing, thumping, chewing, squirming mass, *Homo sapiens* is the only one that makes value judgments about the others. (*Et quis iudicat iudices?*) Even when there's no longer anything to gain by being wary or timorous, we still respond with almost instinctive fear and loathing to a host of things that aren't like us. Sometimes, we flinch not at the reality but at the pictures provided on the Discovery Channel: North America, for example, is not home to the hyena, but the very thought of a scavenger that seems to laugh maniacally as it zeroes in on a meal of carrion evokes a reflexive shiver. The creature, behaving in a way that repels us, is relegated (by all but the most intent zoologists) to the status of a lowlife not deserving our notice, much less our regard.

The hyena's credentials for despicability are easy to understand. So are those of the phylum Arthropoda, especially its insects and arachnids like spiders, chiggers, and ticks. As Annie Dillard says of the insects, they "are not only cold-blooded, and green- and yellow-blooded, but are also cased in a clacking horn. They lack the grace to go about as we do, softside-out to the wind and thorns. They have rigid eyes and brains strung down their backs. . . . No form is too gruesome, no behavior too grotesque." Nor is it simply the otherness of their looks that damns them; they also bite and sting and transport disease.

But, peculiarly, there is a dichotomy between the things that we despise and those that we both loathe and fear. The former often wreak bodily harm, while the latter, though they rarely hurt us, frighten us literally out of our wits, tossing us like toy boats on wild seas of unreason. Why do we simply dislike mosquitoes and poison ivy, which surely cause excruciating itches and blisters, but shudder at snakes, spiders, and centipedes, which would rather flee the scene than attack our kind? We flinch involuntarily not only at the immediate slinking, spinning, lurking presence of such creatures but at the very idea that these monsters occupy room on our planet. Imagination afflicts us as desperately as does reality. The speed, the lack of feet, or their obscene abundance, the fangs and possibilities of venom, the attenuated scaly bodies or the plump hairy ones, the flicking tongues, the multiple eyes—all these characteristics separate the reptiles and arthropods from everything that's sensible and comely. They contradict our notions of the way things ought to be. A phobic reaction sets in: palpitations, sweating palms, a smother of doom that makes the sufferer gasp for air.

Genetic programming may dictate our fear. Not only humankind but all the primates recoil from things like snakes and other sudden apparitions in the trees or grass. The ecologist and natural philosopher Paul Shepard (1925–1996) has written:

No monkey makes light of shapes in the gloom that might be leopards, snakes, or owls. Storms and lightning terrify them. That primal event of the murder story, the scream in the dark, is the primate's ultimate signal of panic. The dark side of imagination generates fearful shapes and bad dreams, infecting shadows with menace, even when the leopards are in fact far away. Such fears are the price of intelligence and the consequences of exposure—the price of sleeping lightly in trees or on cliffs.

H. sapiens, the fiercest primate of all, has fully inherited the ancestral timorousness. It is, as Shepard explains, a protective device that makes for longevity. Our eyes, and those of our simian kin, tell the story. We are diurnal creatures, active in the light of day, and once we were all arboreal, living aloft in the canopy of rain-forest trees. To enable this way of life, evolution equipped the primates with both binocular and color vision, the first to allow accurate estimates of distances to be traversed, the second to tell the difference between bitter green fruit and that which has attained a succulent ripeness. Birds have color vision, but when it comes to furry, infant-suckling mammals, primates are the only ones—with the odd exception of a few rodent species—that are blessed with color vision. But we also see shades of gray. Outside its fovea, the central area that perceives the world in color, the primate retina possesses rod cells that see only in monochrome. Thus, we are able to see not only that there are shadows and nighttime darkness but also what moves—or may at any instant materialize—within the dimness and the dark. What is and what might be—the real leopard and the leopard of imagination—live side by side in the vision of primates. And because we have been designed to expect trouble in the shadows, our actual safety is greatly enhanced.

With snakes, human aversions have been given extra strength by myth and theology: the head of Medusa crowned with writhing, hissing serpents and, worse, all hopes of Eden forever lost. As for the spiders, I have seen it suggested by Richard Conniff that they, too, may be the objects of an aversion "embedded in our genetic memory." Certainly, they, too, are the subjects of myth and folklore: the princess Arachne transformed into a spider because the perfection of her weaving insulted the divine spinster Athena and, on the positive side, the solitary prisoner, like Scotland's fourteenth-century Robert the Bruce, finding a friend in the spider who shares his cell.

The latter view may speak to the difficulty of human rapprochement with eight-leggers; only when there is no other company are spiders to be considered welcome or, at least, ungrudgingly granted tenancy of nearby space. I doubt that the "hundred-leggers," the centipedes, are ever welcome as they skitter across walls and come up suddenly through drains. They share to a hideous excess the spider's fault of too many legs. And they are small enough so that imagination insists on the possibility that they will travel across soft, defenseless skin and invade not just a sleeper's dreams but also the private parts. This perception of the centipede is, in its horrid way, more venomous than the creature's actual bite.

With snakes, spiders, and the whole gaudy, clacking, creeping, many-shaped, and quite uncountable army of the planet's bugs, it's fairly easy to understand the shudder factor. But what of the other living things that people despise: the cowbirds, the poison ivy, and the myriad other bugbears like rats, slugs, crabgrass, jellyfish, and viruses? A good part of despicability comes, of course, from the all-too-real bites, stings, and blisters and from the invisible but equally real frissons and terrors that rise from the collision of other lives with ours. Another clue lies in the very word *bugbear*, which popped up in English in 1581. It referred in its earliest days to things that were spectral and scary—a goblin or a ghost. It still denotes things, real or imaginary, that give rise to a gamut of stressful emotions, ranging from a twinge of annoyance to disabling fear. And *bug* itself, the fourteenth-century word at the heart of *bugbear*, originally designated a phenomenon, usually supernatural, that inspired disturbing physical symptoms, like clammy hands and thumping hearts—symptoms, striking sudden as a lightning bolt, that in themselves exacerbated fright. *Bogeyman* and *bugaboo*: a Black Sabbath of ghoulies and ghosties and long-legged beasties shelter also within these two terms. And to this day, anything we do not understand becomes a bugbear, deserving in its otherness our suspicion and dislike. With a sigh for the idiosyncracies of humankind, however, it should be noted that things that are bugbears to some are beauties to others. The Japanese relish eating kudzu and keep caged crickets as pets, the Chinese consider spiders lucky, and English householders set out nest boxes for starlings. (I've never heard of anyone, however, who admires the tick.)

A species' despicability may also be determined, at least in American minds, by its failure to contribute one jot or tittle to the well-being of our kind. "What is not useful is vicious," wrote Cotton Mather (1663–1728) with the moral certainty of a Puritan who knew beyond all doubt that God had granted man dominion over the fish of the sea, the fowl of the air, the cattle, the creeping things, and every herb bearing seed upon the face of the earth. In this view, a species need not go so far as to harm people; its malice resides in the bare fact that it exists but leads the lily's idle life, neither toiling nor spinning on behalf of those who dominate. The corollary is that the living things that manage to tend to their own instinctual business without getting in our way nonetheless deserve our condemnation and our swats because they do nothing to help us.

This is also the view—*because they are there*—that makes some people shoot at tree swallows flying over the pond just around the corner from my North Carolina home and that leads others to poach carnivorous plants, the sundews and Venus flytraps, from a nearby national forest. It may be said, of course, that there's sport in the first and money in the second. But both reflect relationships turned topsy-turvy. In a world in which the odds were more fairly distributed, the relationship of swallow and gunner, plant and digger would be Zero-Zero, both present in the same place but neither affecting the other in any way. Both gunner and digger would be nothing more than innocent observers—should they even deign to notice bird or plant. But when rifle and spade are wielded, observer turns into predator, and the symbiosis becomes Plus-Minus, with the predator always winning and the prey uprooted or killed outright.

In the stories that follow, the often peculiar relationships of our kind and the species we despise are looked at in their natural, mythic, and literary incarnations. It will be noted that almost every species that we scorn or loathe is superlatively abundant—starlings in their uncountable legions, kudzu in sprawling green tangles that have seized millions of acres, hornworms in every tomato patch and tobacco field, squirrels up every tree. Some of these species are exotic imports that have thrived with grand excess in the United States because the natural controls—the predators and parasites—of their native lands are absent here. Others are indigenous and have always been at home in the New World. But no matter their origin, all are far more ancient in evolutionary terms than we, and all are with us until the end (be it bang or whimper). They may indeed continue to be here, a crawling, flying, leaping horde of survivors, well after we're gone. Howard Ensign Evans, an entomologist who nostalgically remembers stomping tobacco hornworms with his bare feet on his father's farm, offers these words of caution (the italics are mine): "Swatting a mosquito is allowable, considering that mosquitoes are so well able to flood the earth with their kind. *But swat it respectfully*: the mosquito is a product of a million years of evolution." Sue Hubbell, a notable science writer and champion of hexapods, goes so far as to wonder "if we are justified in acting as though we have a *right* to live in an insect-free world." But swat and spray and slaughter as we will, the things we find despicable are well-nigh extermination-proof—with the possible exception of the one species that is peculiarly fitted with the power to self-destruct. As Pogo the 'possum says, "I have seen the enemy, and he is us." But more of this matter in the book's final story.

Along the way, the questions rise like weeds in gardens or mosquitoes from a swamp. Some questions are specific, concerning the lives of particular despicables: How does a centipede manage to run without tripping itself? And how does a cowbird know what it is when the first birds it sees are those of another species? To questions like these, answers may often be found. It turns out that many of the things we despise are, in their own sly ways, quite remarkable.

Other questions are far more obdurate; nor do I propose to attempt to resolve them. The hope is rather to stimulate reflection.

What, for example, might be the rights of that running centipede or the new-hatched cowbird, of a rat or a snake, of jimsonweed or crabgrass? Do rights exist, except as a concept of human devising? To what extent are our lives interlocked with those of the things we despise? To what extent are all the lives on earth interlocked one with another, even at second, third, and fourth removes? Are there lives that the world can do without? Species, genera, whole families whose removal would not cause some cataclysmic wobble in the planet's spin? Why treasure endangered species but scorn the commonplace? Is rarity valuable in and of itself? Might intentional extermination of a species ever be justified? How much is enough? And most vital of all, what means shall we give our children so that they may learn to recognize and delight in the world beyond their finite skins? These questions and others each need a reasoned response, not one that smacks of eco-think, which has a flatulent tendency to come from the gut, not the brain.

Answers are important because of the dilemmas inherent in our attempts to manage our natural surroundings. I think of the good intentions that did in not only the salt-marsh mosquitoes on Florida's Merritt Island but also *Ammodramus maritimus nigrescens*, the dusky subspecies of the seaside sparrow. In the name of human comfort, the marshes were drained to eliminate the mosquitoes' breeding grounds. The hoped-for consequence was achieved: a drastic drop in the mosquito population. But in the wake of that achievement, like an unexpected aftershock, a small bird with a chunky bill, a dark-colored back, and a pale breast heavily streaked with black became extinct because its food supply had disappeared.

We're stuck here, like it or not. So, it behooves us to think hard and well about how we fit into the scheme of things and how we should behave ourselves so that the scheme continues to cohere. As Paul Shepard has said, "What problems and characteristics are in fact uniquely human cannot be clear until we know more about what is not human, and, in discovering what we are not, gain a fresh appreciation of the rich and diverse otherness of the natural world in its own right."

Here, then, are tales of despicable species—mirrors in which we might take a good, long, quizzical look at our most peculiar selves.

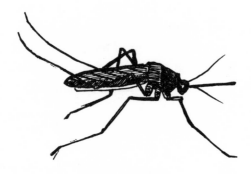

Mosquito (*Culex pipiens*)

PROSPECT AND REFUGE

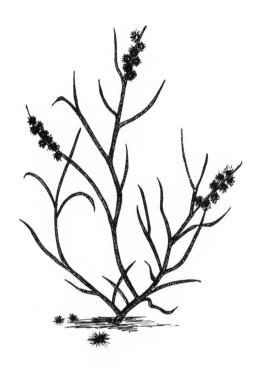

Sandbur (*Cenchrus tribuloides*)

Sandburs

G RASS: imagination conjures an endless panorama of green—sweet new-mown lawns, cattle-cropped pastures, wild prairies where leaves and stems rise tall, then lapse in the wind like waves on the sea. And other colors gleam there, too, the red kernels of Indian corn and the well-sung amber waves of grain. Grass: the word itself rustles and whispers and summons Walt Whitman. The reality of any grassy expanse, be it wild or tame, may be just as appealing as the visions that rise in mind's eye—Spartina, sea oats, tall oats grass, wild rice, maize, rye, bluegrass, red fescue, purple love grass, and a hundred others native to the New World. Grass, nonetheless—as all of us who touch earth know—has its grosser manifestations, like crabgrass, an introduced species, that intrudes in the lawn and insistently nudges aside more modest greenery, and like the native quack grass and nut grass that rage through vegetable patch and flower garden with the swarming, single-minded thrust of a Mongol horde. And at the shore and in disturbed places like roadsides and abandoned fields there grows a kind of grass that is perfectly in balance with its own world but must, by any human reckoning, be considered truly vicious.

Cenchrus tribuloides, "thornlike millet"—I meet it first on Ossabaw Island, Georgia. The group of plants commonly known as millet produces nutritious seeds, which are readily eaten by people, animals, and birds. Cenchrus is Greek for "millet," but this thornlike imposter has simply stolen the millet group's good name and is related only insofar as both belong to the Poaceae, the huge and multifarious grass family, which includes not only lush coverings like bluegrass and fescue, hay crops like timothy, and the economically important cereals that comprise the amber waves, but also gathers in some prickly mistakes (if nature can be said to make mistakes). The only similarities between C. tribuloides and true millet lie in the size and roundness of their seeds. And there all visible resemblance stops.

Ossabaw Island—what a peculiar and time-warped place! It lies off the Georgia coast only twenty short miles from Savannah—

twenty-five thousand acres of sand, tidal marshes, and freshwater ponds, of live oaks swathed in Spanish moss, and huge, fan-leafed palms that rustle and rattle in the sea wind. And it's altogether a more exotic place than any I've seen before, a place in which a peg-legged pirate or even a dinosaur might not seem amiss. I'm here, though, with a gaggle (or perhaps a pride) of writers, editors, and photographers whose special interest is the natural world, particularly as it manifests itself throughout the South. We're here to talk specifically about how being Southerners, by birth or by choice, colors our experience of the land and all that lives thereon. For the weekend of our conversation, we are encamped in somewhat seedy elegance in the palatial Mediterrranean-style house—at least eighteen bedrooms, most with attached baths—that was built as a winter hideaway by Henry Torrey, the Midwestern industrialist who bought the entire island in the 1920s. His daughter, Sandy West, now in her eighties, still lives amid call bells for maids and pantries stocked with glassware and china for dozens of guests. The maids no longer exist, but the guests still arrive, bringing their own food and their own agendas, usually something to do with the arts. In the past several decades, their number has included composers, sculptors, novelists, environmental activists, and the woman who designed Barney the dinosaur. We are simply one small and recent group in a long line of individuals and organizations using the big house as a conference center—and gawking at the strangeness of the sea-island landscape. As is eminently fitting, Ossabaw was sold to Georgia in 1978 and has become the state's first Natural Heritage Preserve.

In 1995, however, the National Trust for Historic Preservation put the island on its list of the country's eleven most endangered places. Long before the 1920s and the incursion of a personal fortune, Ossabaw had lost its claim to being a pristine sea island. From the time that people—the Indians first, then the European explorers and colonists, and later the planters and their slaves—set foot on the sandy beaches, the land and its denizens have been unnaturally altered. Marshlands have been drained and filled, and tide-interrupting causeways built; some woods have been cleared for growing cotton and raising cattle; a web of dirt roads, seventy-five miles altogether, crisscrosses the dunes and swales. An auto graveyard even decorates the island's North End. Much of the original sea-island flora and fauna remains, of course, but has been joined over three hundred years by foreign things. Amid the woods live the gray squirrels and the birds, woodpeckers and warblers, that have always been here, but introduced animals also lay claim today to a not inconsiderable amount of space. White-tailed deer, armadillos, and a great slew of feral pigs, some three thousand of them in many colors from black to rusty red, move with skittish caution through the open underbrush. And Sicilian donkeys, descended from five brought in as pets for Henry Torrey's children, have made themselves wildly at home in the fields and woods. Behind the palatial house, peafowl, geese, black-and-white Muscovy ducks with red wattles, and three horses wander at will, honking, squawking, neighing. One huge coal-black pig dubbed Lucky has become a permanent hanger-on, dining well on kitchen scraps. Half-grown wild piglets hover on the fringes of the action hoping that some food will be spilled for them. I see Sandy West out back in the early morning refilling feed and water buckets. Despite her years, she works with youthful verve and vigor.

But some things on Ossabaw are immemorial. The name is said to mean "yaupon holly bushes' place," and the yaupons still grow here in thriving numbers. Nor do they at all resemble the flourishing but spindly shrubs I know on the Carolina coast; they have attained the status of true trees and boast solid, mottled gray-green trunks that may measure as much as a full foot in diameter. The live oaks, some growing naturally and others planted more than two hundred years ago, are as gnarled as the trees in any enchanted woods conjured by the Brothers Grimm. I see one oak, huge and decaying but still almost fully decked out with glossy dark green leaves, that first poked its head up through the soil some six hundred years ago, around the time that Columbus set sail. Snakes—rat snakes, king snakes, and black racers, rattlesnakes and copper-heads—lurk and slither everywhere as they always have, while alligators haunt the sloughs, bald eagles soar overhead, and shore-birds—willets, yellow-legged sandpipers, and the tiny, hard-to-tell-apart sandpiper species collectively known as "peeps"—run and peck through the sands at water's edge.

And here on the beaches and dunes—like a thorn on a rose, like a serpent's tooth—*C. tribuloides* also makes itself at home. The sands of Ossabaw, and those of its sister sea islands, like Saint Catherines, Blackbeard, and Sapelo, were not designed with human comfort as a prime consideration. Beachcombing is best accomplished in a pair of shoes or boots, and even then there's no escaping the long-spined burs, which will insinuate themselves into the waffle treads of the soles. That's how I first discover them. After the morning efforts to define Southern nature writers (if they are definable), we make an early afternoon excursion to South Beach. And here I am, sitting on a handy tree stump to watch the various acrobatics of a kingfisher and an immature bald eagle, but when I cross my legs, hoisting left ankle over right knee, the hand used for the hoisting is right smartly punctured by the burs stuck in my soles. Burgrass! Sandbur! Sandspur! The common names for this common plant hiss and spit in their own right and make for excellent invective. The half-hour ride back to the palatial house is spent gingerly extracting needle-sharp sandburs from the soles of my shoes. I save some for further study by sticking them on my shirt, where they cling unbudgeably till they are put into a pint-sized plastic freezer bag. And even that is not enough to keep them from pricking and stabbing; though the bag has been folded around them, the rigid spines, packed as thickly as those on a sea urchin and each at least a centimeter long, have readily pierced three layers of tough plastic.

After the outing, I go to the back yard and take pictures of the half-grown wild piglets that are hanging around hoping for crumbs.

When they cotton to my presence, they glance at me with quick suspicion and scoot. Then people gather again beside giant yaupons to continue exploring this entity dubbed the Southern nature writer. The discussions ramble and rage. Some of the talk is profoundly silly, especially in the attempts to define ourselves in relation to Westerners: Westerners see things, Southerners see characters; the West is geological, the South biological. But two of our number come close to definitions that have the ring of truth. One says, "We are an endangered species. We still have a sense of place." And the other, "There are things we see in a landscape—prospect and refuge. We as writers are nurtured by a sense of the past." He will tell me later that the notion of prospect and refuge is not original with him but rather comes out of a theory about how our feelings of beauty and fitness in landscape reflect our deep Darwinian past, when we needed both a point of vantage and a place of concealment if we were to succeed, on the one hand, in eating and, on the other, in not being eaten.

Prospect and refuge, vantage and safe shelter—I latch on to these, along with a picture of Southern writers being rocked like babies in the cradle of the past. But it's not only the past that nurtures us. We are nurtured also by trumpet creepers, longleaf pines, alligators, and a folk memory of ivory-billed woodpeckers. Sustenance comes, too, in beaches and salt marshes on the flat-as-a-flounder coast, it comes in Appalachian peaks and hollows—and all of it well steamed and stewed in a cauldron of hot, humid summers. There's much to consider, from eagles and azaleas to feral pigs and the peculiar thornlike millet.

As I learn later, the genus *Cenchrus* consists of about twenty-five species, most of them native to the New World's tropics. It is indeed a common plant—a common scourge—fond of sandy soil and quick to injure the unwary. Nor are all of its models confined to warmer regions; three are widely found in North America, and one—*C. longispinus*, "long-spined millet"—spreads across the continent. This long-spined sort may be found in disturbed areas, like roadsides and vacant lots, from New Hampshire to Oregon, south through the Carolinas and Georgia, and west through Texas into New Mexico. Its usual mode of growth is to sprawl, hugging the ground unobtrusively in what might seem an effort at going unnoticed, at hiding its great piercing power. *C. tribuloides*, its thornlike cousin, is the species usually damned as a "sandspur," and, from Staten Island to Florida, it is to be found with truly pestiferous abundance on the dunes and beaches of the Atlantic coast, including those at my home beach, Great Neck Point. "Those miserable little monkeys"—that's how a neighbor describes them. How I have missed a painful encounter in the years of my residence beside the wide and salty river Neuse, I do not know—fool luck, perhaps. Of the trio of pseudomillets thriving in North America, the third is *C. incertus*, "uncertain millet," which may be named for its wont to start out as an annual plant growing in a tall upright clump but then to dig in, when fortune brings the right weather and nutrients, and transform itself into a perennial.

Burgrass! Sandbur! Sandspur! These stubborn plants inspire not just ordinary folk but also botanists to lose their objectivity. Usually, the latter deploy sobersided technical terms like these used in *Gray's New Manual of Botany* to describe the prickery, stickery seed pods of *C. tribuloides:* "Spikelets 1-flowered, acuminate, 2–6 together, subtended by a short-pediceled ovoid or globular involucre of rigid connate spines." But listen to these judgments in two field guides. With laudable restraint, the one identifying shore plants calls thornlike millet "Unpleasant to walk on barefooted!" The other, a volume devoted to grasses, goes all out to say this of the long-spined variety: "Horribly spiny flower clusters, extremely painful to step on." Granted, these guides were written to satisfy popular curiosity, but only in describing *Cenchrus* species do they forfeit objectivity and utter a loud, sharp yelp. It's fair to suspect that both attest to excruciating personal encounters with unpleasant, horrible things that look like tiny morning stars bristling with a hundred spikes.

I spy another difference between Southerners and Westerners. While the former would surely rank sandburs high on any list of despicable weeds, the latter might nominate puncture vine, which has reached the status of a pest in places like Arizona, New Mexico, and West Texas. With a habit of prostrate growth and a nutlet with two stout, sharp-pointed spines that jut out like the horns of a steer, it is capable of doing serious harm not only to bare feet but to bicycle tires and the mouths of grazing livestock. The formal name of this well-defended plant is *Tribulus terrestris*, "earth thorn," and it belongs to the Zygophyllaceae, the caltrop family, which includes other thorn-studded species like the star thistles and pests like the knapweeds, along with such gardeners' favorites as bachelor's button and dusty miller. But puncture vine is not a grass, nor is it native to the New World but came as a stowaway from the Mediterranean.

The sandburs have been here from the beginning. The burs are really nothing more than coverings for seeds. Like chestnuts protected within a densely prickery pod, sweet gum seeds within a thorny ball, and cockleburs within a horrid palisade of barbed spines, the seeds of *Cenchrus* hide behind armor. Bur and seed together constitute the fruit. But why build such a fortress? Two reasons present themselves, and the first is protection: to keep the fruits from being devoured and digested, never to have a chance at sprouting. It has been noted that cattle and sheep avoid eating these plants, even when they are young and easy to chew. The second reason is transport: to stick tightly in fur, hair, flesh, and shoes so that the seeds and, with them, the next generations of *Cenchrus* are dispersed as widely as possible. Prospect and refuge—these are not only human goals but those of *Cenchrus* also: ensuring the future and shielding its tender imminence.

As we leave Ossabaw, I see a tiny pig—red as Georgia clay from snout to tail—streaking across the road that leads to the dock and the boat that will ferry us back to the mainland. Along with the sandburs, it encapsulates for me the secret of Ossabaw. Not just the people who write on the intricate peculiarities of nature but every last one of us needs some old-time prickliness, along with a good dash of upstart, feral notions, in the underbrush of our imaginations.

Razorback Hog

THE BARKINGS OF A
JOYFUL SQUIRREL

Gray Squirrel (*Sciurus carolinensis*)

Gray Squirrel

WHEN I press Dick Coleman, my doctor, for the reason he finds squirrels the most despicable species on earth, he says, "Because they're stupid, that's why."

I've always thought of Eastern gray squirrels as fat, sassy tail-twitchers, as admirably fearless acrobats (I have no head for heights), and as infinitely clever thieves able to get the better of any bird feeder. With great wit and no little accuracy, a friend calls them the monkeys of North America. Squirrels are also good to eat—if they're cooked so that they retain some of their juices rather than being fried until the meat is nothing but dry, leathery strips wrapped around tiny bones. Brunswick stew—hurray! And I think of other squirrels, not our familiar gray species nor the tree-dwelling kind in general but rather the playful creatures that romp through human imagination—among them, Rocky Squirrel, the bucktoothed side-kick of Bullwinkle Moose in the 1960s cartoons, and Beatrix Potter's classic Squirrel Nutkin, an English red squirrel, brother of Twinkle-berry and neighbor to Peter Rabbit and Mrs. Tiggy-Winkle the hedgehog. And at Mary Baldwin, a small liberal arts college for women located in Virginia, the sports teams, volleyball to soccer, call themselves the Squirrels. Altogether, be they four-legged or human, real or imaginary, squirrels are entertaining and inspira-tional, not to mention delicious. In just what ways can they possibly be stupid?

"They pile up nuts," Dick says with a *hmpf*, "and they bury them. Then they forget where they put them. Every year, those durn animals tear up my yard looking for nuts."

So squirrels can wreak costly havoc in suburban landscaping. I've also been told that, sneaking in through vents beneath the eaves, they can tear up an attic as efficiently as they do a lawn. Nei-ther of these reasons, however, sits at the top of the list for despising them. The complaint heard most often comes from back-yard bird-watchers, who sputter and fume about another kind of expensive wreckage: the ongoing, undeterrable theft of bird seed and the con-sequent destruction of feeders. As it turns out, Dick has complaints in that department, too: "Squirrels! They mess with the sunflower seed put on the ground by the woodpeckers. Squirrels, chipmunks, doves, it's a zoo under the feeders."

What kind of creature is this gray squirrel that causes such condemnation and outrage in humankind?

A rodent, that's what. First cousin to the flying squirrels and ground squirrels; kin at only a slight remove to mice, rats, and voles, beavers and porcupines. All are members of the order Rodentia, a Latin word that means "gnawers." And all have notable incisors, enamel in front, dentine in back, which are not rooted in the jaw but continue to grow throughout the animal's life. Lest they become so long that they keep the animal from feeding properly, such teeth must be frequently filed down, a task accomplished, of course, by chomping into whatever's handy—a tree for dam building, the husk of a succulent nut, the rafters and stored goods in an attic, the bird feeder in the back yard. (Mice, which always make themselves at home in our North Carolina trailer during the winter, have planted their incisors not only into candles and soup-can labels but also into the stove's pink fiberglass insulation, which they've used to line the nests located in sundry drawers. And once upon a time, a gray squirrel sank its teeth into my tomatoes, still green on the vine, but more about that later.) Gnawing sharpens the teeth by quickly wearing away the soft dentine and leaving a well-honed cutting edge on the hard anterior enamel.

In the next zoological subdivision, that of family, the squirrels belong to the Sciuridae, which means simply "squirrelkind." The Latin word for squirrel is *sciurus*. It occurs in the work of Martial, the Roman poet, and that of his contemporary, the naturalist Pliny, in the first century A.D.; the squirrels to which they refer, however, are European species, not the gray squirrel, a native of North America that was introduced into the Old World only in the last hundred years.

Squirrelkind is further divided into three groups: tree, flying, and ground squirrels. The last group denotes the burrowers—the chipmunks and woodchucks of the Eastern United States, the prairie dogs of the central plains, the marmots of the Rockies, and at least twenty species of striped ground squirrels. (Burrower though it be, I have, however, seen a woodchuck huff and chuff its way up a tree to make a desperate—and successful—high-rise escape from my dog.) The flying squirrels are huge-eyed creatures of the night that leave their cavity nests after dark to glide in search of nuts, grains, blossoms, insects, and occasionally birds' eggs. My favorite early observer of the natural scene, John Lawson, surveyor general to the lords proprietors of the Carolinas, published this description of airborne squirrelkind in 1709:

> He has not Wings, as Birds or Bats have, there being a fine thin Skin cover'd with Hair, as the rest of the parts are. This is from the Fore-Feet to the Hinder-Feet, which is extended and holds so much Air, as buoys him up, from one Tree to another, that are greater distances asunder than other Squirrels can reach by jumping or springing. He is made very tame, is an Enemy to a Cornfield (as all Squirrels are) and eats only the germinating Eye of the Grain, which is very sweet.

Today, while the Southern flying squirrel thrives, the Northern species, not uncommon in the northern United States and Canada, is so hard to find below the Mason-Dixon line that it has been listed in several states as threatened or endangered.

The tree squirrels of the East are three in number: Eastern red, Eastern gray, and fox. The fox, the giant among them, is formally named *Sciurus niger*, "black squirrel," for the black face it sometimes displays on its otherwise gray self; many that are resident in the North, however, wear rusty pelts. The pipsqueak is the red squirrel, *Tamiasciurus hudsonicus*, which means "Hudson's housekeeper squirrel"; its Western cousins, the spruce squirrel, *T. fremonti*, and the chickaree, *T. douglasii*, also bear scientific names that honor intrepid nineteenth-century explorers—respectively, Colonel John Charles Frémont, who shared an expedition to California with Kit Carson, and David Douglas, the Scottish plant collector, who is honored also in the common name of the Douglas fir. The Eastern red squirrel, a highly territorial beast, chatters at any creature, human or otherwise, that invades it chosen realm. I do not see it on the low-lying Carolina coast, but in the wooded town park where once I walked the dog during our Virginia winters, its dry, querulous bark was a constant as we made our rounds. The middle-sized gray squirrel—the one deemed stupid by my doctor—is formally known as *Sciurus carolinensis*, the Carolina squirrel, but it ranges widely in the Eastern United States, from New England southward. And it seems, in my observations at any rate, that as one goes farther south, the species gets noticeably smaller. It is large and bold in Connecticut and New York; I've seen typical specimens, many of them melanistic, all nearly as big and furry as Persian cats, romping through the Brooklyn Botanic Gardens. But in the Shenandoah Valley, though still hearty, the species is reduced in heft by perhaps a quarter, and on the Carolina coast, it's a puny little thing. Some that I see often in our riverside yard belong to a clan with a genetic predisposition for bushy blond tails, but all the gray squirrels that sport in our sweet gums and loblolly pines are such little things, more bones than meat, that I'd hesitate to put them in a pot of Brunswick stew.

In the seventeenth century, when Europeans first began to colonize these wild shores where prodigious hardwood forests and piney woods stretched ever westward, gray squirrels were even more abundant, more ubiquitous than they are today. But between that time and the earliest years of the twentieth century, they were almost extirpated. Their numbers had been so reduced that some doubted the species would survive. Several reasons account for the disastrous diminishment of gray squirrel populations. One was loss of habitat as the unbroken aboriginal forests fell to the ax. A second reason, just as important and equally fatal, was that noted by John Lawson: like its flying cousins, the gray squirrel was, is, and ever shall be an "Enemy to a Cornfield." The animal's sweet tooth was nearly its undoing, for bounties were widely handed out by sore-beset farmers for the carcasses that shooters brought in. In 1748, Peter Kalm, the Swedish plant collector, noted in his journal that in Maryland everyone was required to kill four squirrels yearly and to present their heads "to a local officer to prevent deceit."

Kalm also reported an imaginative rumor, circulating among Pennsylvanians:

> Squirrels are the chief food of the rattlesnake and other snakes, and it is a common fancy with the people hereabouts that when the rattlesnake lies on the ground and fixes its eyes upon a squirrel, the latter will be as if charmed, and that though it be on the uppermost branches of a tree it will come down by degrees until it leaps into the snake's mouth. The snake then licks the little animal several times and makes it wet all over with his spittle so that it may go down the throat easier. It then swallows the whole squirrel at once.

But snakes, no matter how hearty their appetites, could never have accounted for the demise of many squirrels.

Along with dwindling forests and slaughter for money, I see a third reason for plummeting populations: the eternal human fondness for sport, in which people go hunting not to obtain necessary victuals but rather to show off their marksmanship. *Bang!*—the Carolina parakeets and the sky-darkening flights of passenger pigeons fall to earth forever. *Bang!*—the Eastern elk are extirpated, the shaggy, thunderous herds of bison also disappear from Appalachian valleys and from the Great Plains as well. *Bang!*—the gray squirrel came within a whisker of joining them in whatever heaven is reserved for animals.

It may be, however, that squirrel shooting—for whatever reason, money or sport—helped Americans beat the British in the Revolutionary War. In the early days, when this country was still a collection of colonies, its people developed long, lean rifles for hunting small game. Slimmed to 40- to 50-calibers, using lighter balls and less powder than traditional muskets, these flintlocks could outshoot the typical British weapon three yards to one and not only that but do so with winning accuracy.

The squirrel as denizen of the woods, the squirrel as fancier of corn, and the squirrel as target pop up frequently in the writings of John James Audubon, who wielded a gun as skillfully as he did a paintbrush. In one of his eclectic "Episodes," which are short, wonderfully pictorial—though frequently overinventive or downright mendacious—essays on people and events, he notes that, like the cunning raccoon, the squirrel knows "when the corn is juicy and pleasant to eat." In another, he contrasts the bleakness of camping on the granite coast of Labrador with the pleasures of doing the same thing in Mississippi, where, despite heat and mosquitoes, "the barkings of a joyful Squirrel, or the notes of the Barred Owl, that grave buffoon of our western woods, never fail to gladden the camper." Then, in an Episode entitled "Kentucky Sports," Audubon's talent for invention enters jauntily when he speaks of another kind of barking:

> *Barking off Squirrels* is a delightful sport, and in my opinion requires a greater degree of accuracy than any other. I first witnessed this manner of procuring squirrels whilst near the town of Frankfort. The performer was the celebrated Daniel Boone. We . . . followed the margins of the Kentucky River, until we reached a piece of flat land thickly covered with black walnuts, oaks, and hickories. As the general mast was a good one that year, Squirrels were seen gambolling on every tree around us. My companion, a stout, hale, and athletic man, dressed in a homespun hunting shirt, bare-legged and moccasined, carried a long and heavy rifle, . . . which he hoped would not fail on this occasion, as he felt proud to show me his skill. The gun was wiped, the powder measured, the ball patched with six-hundred-thread linen, and the charge sent home with a hickory rod. We moved not a step from the place, for the Squirrels were so numerous that it was not necessary to go after them.

The fiction here is Audubon's claim to acquaintance with Boone, fifty years his senior, who would have been doddering, or close to it, at the time of this purported encounter. But the squirrel-hunting method that he describes is nothing less than gospel truth. The hunter did not set each squirrel directly in his sights but rather aimed at the bark just below the point at which the animal clung to a tree. When the ball hit, the bark was "shivered into splinters." It was the mighty concussion that killed the squirrel, which then fell undamaged to the ground. The barking technique was designed to avoid shivering the squirrels themselves into splinters. And so a day of hunting would proceed, squirrel after squirrel after squirrel, as many as the gunners wished. (I wonder how many ended up in pots of Brunswick stew.) Dick, my doctor, would surely have lauded their prodigiously successful efforts.

After hitting a low point in the early 1900s, *S. carolinensis* has recovered nicely from onslaughts of sportsmen like Audubon and Boone. The new lease on life, however, is not so much accounted for by a loss of human interest in hunting for the sake of hunting as by the imposition of hunting seasons and limits and, more, by the protection and restoration of Eastern woodlands, the gray squirrel's necessary high-rise habitat. State parks and game commissions, national forests, private organizations promoting conservation—all have served to pull back the joyful barker from the brink of doom.

The wanton squirrels that blithely eat the farmers' corn, frolic through the trees in plain sight of shooters, or dig endless divots out of Dick Coleman's yard—are they stupid? Hardly, nor does stupidity figure at all in the equation. The animals are simply predisposed to be there, collecting, eating, storing food, be it given by nature or planted by man. The cleverness of squirrels, though, is well worth noting.

And clever they are, demonstrably so. A two-part documentary film called *Daylight Robbery*, made several years ago in England, shows gray squirrels outwitting the most contortive human attempts to thwart their raids on bird feeders. In that land, the gray squirrel is an invader, an exotic import that, since its arrival a century ago, has taken over much of the native red squirrel's territory. Squirrel Nutkin, his brother Twinkleberry, and their small, talkative red-brown kind have suffered conquest and a great reduction in number. So it's not just raids by gray squirrels—"tree rats," as some would have it—that rile the human population but their displacement of a species hallowed by Beatrix Potter and as lovable, if not so mythic, as Eeyore, Piglet, and Winnie-the-Pooh (not to mention Rat and Mole). The feeders built to foil attack by marauding foreigners were equipped with a multitude of ingenious devices: baffles that tilted and windmills that spun under the squirrel's weight, lines strung with rotating disks, tubes and tunnels, and a rocket-shaped sled that had to be mounted and ridden before the goal could be won. En route to the feeder, the squirrel sometimes had to make gargantuan leaps between one station and the next. The feeder itself was placed so that no access was possible other than that through this obstacle course more daunting than any in boot camp. Did victory elude the squirrel? Of course not. Winning through would take several attempts, but the bird-seed prize was inevitably seized, gnawed, and digested. Gray squirrels are not only clever; they possess a fierce determination and a considerable aptitude for problem solving.

Two decades ago, I watched a gray squirrel work its way through the mechanics of a special problem—that of taking one of my green tomatoes up a tree. I lived then in the basement apartment of an 1840s house built on the side of a steep hill in the small Virginia town of my growing up. The apartment's location in the basement does not, however, mean that it is subterranean; instead, through windows six feet high, the living-dining room gives a fine view of the steeply downsloping back yard. And in that yard (where once I found kudzu stealthily sprouting up and stretching out), I'd made a garden to ease my annual craving for homegrown tomatoes, red-ripe and sweetened by the sun. The garden attracted thieves. One, not surprising, was my landlady, but I hadn't expected the squirrel. I became aware of its activities one noon as I stood in the kitchen fixing a double-thick BLT for lunch. The kitchen overlooks the side yard, but its window is also a six-footer that frames a tall tree. I no longer recall what kind of tree it is—it's still very much there, and I could go look—but its identity is not so important as the memory of the blue jays that built a rickety stick-nest in the lower branches one spring and let me watch them hatch and fledge their young. And certainly not so important as the memory of the astounding acrobatics executed by that squirrel as it attempted to carry a fresh-picked green tomato up the trunk. Time after time, it made a flying leap upward, grabbed the bark with its cling-fast claws, and tried for the top at full speed. Time after time, the green tomato, a good bit larger than the squirrel's head, acted as a weight that loosened the claws, swung the animal around one hundred and eighty degrees, and sent it lickety-split back to the ground. To the rescue: cleverness, determination, and a keen ability to solve food-related conundrums. And how was the job of getting tomato from ground to the leafy heights accomplished? The squirrel ascended the tree backward—tail first, tomato last. Without futile preliminaries, similar ascents were made the next day and the day after. It may have been the one of the smallest circuses on earth, but what grand entertainment, and all for the price of a few green tomatoes! The depredations of the landlady (my tomatoes but *her* back yard) were far more serious.

By now it must be clear that squirrels, at least to my way of thinking, are anything but despicable. And I'm sure that even those thousands of people who truly, deeply detest them will acknowledge that they play a not insignificant role in the scheme of things. In fact, they're part of a win-win symbiosis: just as trees serve squirrels, providing them with food, shelter, nesting materials, exercise, and safety from earthbound creatures (or those, at least, that do not carry guns), so squirrels serve trees by practicing reforestation. If not for those nuts that they store but forget about or fail to find despite the most intensive digging, the Eastern United States would be less thickly covered with black walnuts, the many kinds of oaks, and a multitude of different hickories, including the pecan.

Villains? Vaudevillians? Something else? Whatever gray squirrels really are, we tend to see them mainly as their lives impinge on ours. In that respect, I must grant that on occasion they're nuisances, teasing dogs with malice aforethought, bombarding passersby with sticks and acorns (the very missiles that Squirrel Nutkin, grown irritable with age, hurled down from his tree). But if the critters invade and tear up attics, if they work mischief on yards and feeders, it's surely because we ourselves have presented them with opportunities that their inborn squirrelness cannot resist. Problems like those of Dick Coleman—the dug-up lawn, the zoo under the feeders—aren't problems at all to the teeming, tail-flicking hordes of *S. carolinensis* that wreak the damage. They're simply taking full advantage of the circumstances in which they find themselves.

Dick's wife, Jan, has taken to trapping and transporting squirrels. Alas, though that strategy bears short-term satisfaction, it's tantamount to commanding the tides not to roll in. Remove one squirrel, another—maybe two—will take its place. But, for what it's worth, I have a cure for squirrel-wrought devastation. Bird feeders should, of course, be banished altogether. Then, lawn and bordering beds of shrubs and flowers should be converted into pavement or, more aesthetically pleasing, a Japanese garden unsuitable for burying nuts: rocks, carefully raked sand, greenery that does not furnish squirrel food, and a pond with lily pads and bullfrogs. The damage worked by the frogs would be minimal, and if their population should explode, well, frogs' legs are almost as good to eat as Brunswick stew.

Ah, Brunswick stew! By way of a coda to this inquiry into the nature of the gray squirrel, here is the old-fashioned but eminently usable recipe handed on by my grandmother, Jannette, for whom I was named (and, yes, my name sports all those extra letters, but for reasons of laziness I do not use them). Her father, a medal-winning marksman, spent much time in the field, and to commemorate his exploits, his wife, my great-grandmother, designed and worked a large piece of filet crochet that shows him in deerstalker and hunting breeches, rifle on his shoulder and hound dog at his side. The piece, mounted on brown velvet and framed, is now displayed in my upstairs hall.

End of divagation. Here's the recipe. For the conservative palate, chicken may be substituted.

JANNETTE EAST'S BRUNSWICK STEW

3 squirrels, skinned and cut into pieces
1 gallon water

- Boil till meat comes off bones. Chop meat fine after removing bones. Put back into the same water. Add:
  ¼ pound lean country bacon, chopped fine
  1 quart Irish potatoes, sliced thin or cut in squares
  ½ quart lima beans, fresh or dried soaked in water and split
  1 quart tomatoes, peeled and cut
  1 large onion, chopped
  ½ teaspoon Worcestershire sauce
  salt and pepper to taste

- Boil gently for 5 hours. As water boils down renew with hot water and stir often to prevent burning. Add:
  6 ears corn
  ½ pound butter

- Cook until corn is done and butter is melted.

NOTES FOR THE CONTEMPORARY COOK:

1. Cooking time may be reduced from 5 to 2½ hours. The secret is to keep the ingredients at a constant and *gentle* simmer.
2. Cut the kernels off the corn and add them, not the cobs, to the stew. Frozen corn may be substituted.
3. The butter may be eliminated, for the country bacon will provide enough fat for smoothness and flavor.

4. As accompaniments, serve my grandmother's favorites: biscuits and butter, a tossed green salad, and, for dessert, devil's food cake or lemon meringue pie.

5. As Audubon might have said, *Bon appétit.*

MURMURATIONS

Starling (*Sturnus vulgaris*)

European Starling

APRIL: a sudden eviction has occurred in the new living quarters located in a tall pine snag near the wide and salty river Neuse. For the last two years, the snag has served as a high-rise condo for woodpeckers. Excavating a fresh new hole midway down the weathered, barkless trunk each year, a pair of pileated woodpeckers has nested deep within the dead wood. Early this April, yellow-shafted flickers took up residence in the pileateds' old quarters, and red-bellied woodpeckers drilled out a completely new apartment in the uppermost level of the snag, at a juncture that is marked by the silvery stubs of three broken-off branches.

It was, in fact, the red-bellied male that alerted me to the new apartment in the first place. For several days I'd heard him drumming and trilling, trilling and drumming. I knew what bird he was by his cry, which is not the whistle or skriek typical of other woodpeckers, and certainly not the lunatic cackle of the pileateds, but rather a rapid, throaty, sweet-ringing music. Of course, I went to see if I could find him. And there he was, clinging to the snag, propped on his stiff-feathered tail, mere inches from a hole with freshly chipped edges. As I watched, he slipped inside. During the next week, I listened and watched, found the year's other woodpeckers, and kept an eye on the whole community. The pair of pileateds spelled each other; sometimes his head, sometimes, hers, bold and red-crested, would be visible in the entrance to their nest. The flickers were cagey, seldom allowing themselves to be seen; their comings and goings were given away mainly by small, downy feathers caught on the rough wood of their doorway. All the while, the male red-belly put himself on display near the tip of the snag.

It may have been the red-belly's musical presence that attracted the rude attentions of the small, swart, pushy stranger. Or perhaps the stranger's dark eye was simply drawn to a handy-looking hole. Whatever the reason, eviction ensued. It was swift and merciless, nor could it be appealed. The stranger was a starling, of course, a bird notorious for throwing out legitimate tenants and moving right in. Within an hour, he began furnishing the cavity with pine straw.

His diligence soon lured a mate, who helped him put the finishing touches on interior decoration and then settled in to lay her eggs. As his kind does (and some other kinds as well), he guarded her jealously and at the same time copulated with other females every chance he could get. He may even have found a second mate and established another household.

Late May: the secretive flickers leave no trace of their nesting failure or success, but the pileateds fledge at least three young, two of them red-mustached males. After the red-bellies' dispossession, I often saw them drumming near the snag and heard their trills; the appearance of young birds testifies to a triumph over the forces of darkness. As for those forces, the soot-brown bodies of fledglings mingle with black adult bodies to crowd the three silvery branch stubs at the top of the snag. And there they perch, announcing themselves with wheezes and sighs.

Sturnus vulgaris, the European starling—this is the bird that North Americans love to despise. Indeed, we seem to despise it above all other avian species, even the house sparrow and the rock dove. (The latter is the euphemistic name applied by ornithologists to ordinary pigeons.) The starling regularly dispossesses birds that people consider more attractive—not just woodpeckers but other cavity nesters, like bluebirds, titmice, the golden prothonotary warblers, and the great crested flycatchers, which are feathered in cinnamon and lemon. It even competes for space with cavity- and box-nesting wood ducks. Nor are its raids on the territory of other species confined to the natural world. It also drives city folk to desperation by soiling buildings as thoroughly as pigeons do; it enrages farmers, impoverishes them, by wreaking havoc on fruit and grain crops. It behaves like a ghostly intruder, invisible and frightening; it has figured at least once in rumors of diabolic practices. It provoked my peaceable, nature-loving father into picking up his gun.

My father's long-ago market-garden farm in Ohio: I remember that he toted a shotgun as he led me to a crab-apple tree halfway up the dirt lane, past the storage barn where horsedrawn ploughs, harrows, wagons, and hay balers were kept, along with a mess of wooden barrels for making vinegar. The season must have been late fall or early winter, for the tree was leafless. The branches, however, were far from bare. Black birds no bigger than my child-sized fist had perched themselves wing to wing on almost every available limb and twig. They were thick as cockleburs; they hunched and glowered; softly, they jeered. I knew they were bad birds before my father introduced them. "Starlings," he said. "Stay back, honey. I'll show them." And he fired. Darkness fell from the tree in small feathered clots. But most of the flock simply wheeled upward with a slap of wings and flew away. After counting the fallen, my father explained that starlings showed no mercy, working intolerable damage on his cherries and plums, pears and peaches—the dang birds invited being shot. The air did not clear. I knew even then that my sense of something bad resided not so much in the birds themselves and their unlovely irruption into a child's awareness as in my father's lethal response to their presence. It wasn't until I was older than he'd ever lived to be that my brother, who'd read his farming daybooks, made me privy to more information: with that old shotgun, an Iver Johnson .410, he had not only regularly blasted down starlings but kept meticulous records on the number of victims. Worse, he'd compounded the crime by mounting the same kind of determined campaign against house sparrows.

Starlings, however, are not protected anywhere in the United States. As one species in an unholy trinity that includes the house sparrow and the pigeon, the bird is considered open game, up for slaughter in any season. State laws may apply to all three, nonetheless, with a hunting license required for would-be bird plinkers, or a special permit for scientists who aim to trap, collect, and study them. But these pariahs—who springs to their defense? Will animal-rights activists ever mount campaigns to protect them? The success of any such movements would surely be doomed at the outset: the unlovely three are too many to count, while their partisans are few. What good are they anyway?

In particular, what good are starlings? Apart, that is, from being good to themselves in the highly successful perpetuation of their own squat, sooty kind? But, though the bird does not, and never will, muster much human support, it has also proved useful to us, albeit in tiny and peculiar ways. It is ornamental: in Europe, people intentionally attract starlings to their yards by erecting nest boxes. It helps anglers: in Britain, the feathers, taken from birds shot in their winter roosts, are using in tying fishing flies. It is edible: the bodies of the plucked birds are sent to the Continent and turned into paté. And *S. vulgaris*, though vulgar indeed, has been downright inspirational: not only did it provoke two—not one but *two*—compositions from Mozart, who kept a caged starling as a pet, but it has also provided an image for W. H. Auden and served as a muse to John Updike, from whom it called forth a fine poem. But more later about the music and the poems, and about a more recent starling project that has been awarded a grant form the Minnesota State Arts Board.

What good are starlings to the greater world, the world that encompasses both them and us? Are they required in the scheme of things? A necessary presence without which the links connecting all life on earth would be irremediably severed? Would their absence create a slow leak in earth's substance? Would it make a hole, a void, into which everything else would be sucked, vanishing forever?

All the starlings on earth—and they are legion—got off to an innocuous start. The family, with twenty-four genera and more than one hundred species, is the Sturnidae, which means simply "starlingkind." The family name comes from the Latin *sturnus*, the word that Romans used to designate the starling most familiar to the Western world, the bird that science has denominated *vulgaris*, or "common." The family includes the mynahs along with a varied batch of drab, compact, slim-billed birds that bear a close family resemblance to the European starlings we know (which are arguably the drabbest of the lot) and also many others that sport colorful feathers—rose, violet, glossy purple, vibrant orange, yellow, green, or white—that people use for their own adornment. Some of the common names speak of this splendor: golden-breasted starling, violet-backed starling, red-winged, red-browed, and rose-colored starlings. Some of these birds wear crests, others grow wattles, and the several Asian species, in particular, feature patches of bare skin around the eyes. Though most species nest in holes, some are choosy, preferring holes located in cliffs or behind waterfalls, while others like to dig out their own cavities in muddy banks or drill them, woodpeckerlike, in dead trees. A few, however, actually build nests that are cup-shaped or domed. Many starlings lay spotted eggs, though eggs laid by members of the genus *Sturnus* are generally spotless and pale. And, except for the Antarctic, starlingkind has made itself at home all over the world. Our bird, the European starling, may be found not only throughout Western Europe and the United States, including Alaska's Arctic north, but also in places as far-flung as Iran and Siberia, Egypt and the Madeira Islands, not to mention all the regions in between. It has been introduced into South Africa and Australia. It was the very first species I saw as my plane came in for a landing in New Zealand (the second and third species were also birds that had been transported for reasons of sentiment from their native lands: the house sparrow and the mallard).

European starling—that is the occasionally ornamental, sometimes useful, peculiarly inspiring, ubiquitous, plaguey bird that will inhabit this story from here on. Its everyday name might seem a chiding acknowledgment of the source of North America's infestation. But, no, the name is not reserved solely for exasperated use by people living on the west side of the Atlantic; it's heard throughout Europe, too. Another geographic term would have been more accurate: the starling we know best, along with its numerous kin, probably originated in southeast Asia. And there, in its earliest incarnations, it was likely an arboreal bird that sipped nectar, ate fruit and pollen, and snacked on the insects that were also attracted to the feast in the trees. Some of the Asian species still lead elevated lives, but members of the genus *Sturnus* have notably descended to the ground. Though they have hardly forsaken their passion for fruit, their dinners more often consist of grubs and other insect delicacies harbored in the soil. Clever birds, they long ago spotted and learned to exploit an underused subterranean larder.

Part of the European starling's success in colonizing our country coast to coast has to do with its ability to find buried treasure. Its preferred locations for foraging are open places with short vegetation, like pastures grazed by livestock and closely manicured lawns. The technique is this: insert closed bill into ground, open mandibles, probe for and find grub, shut bill on prey, and withdraw it forthwith. Meanwhile, between captures, a feeding bird will strut on the grass, engage in leapfrog with comrades, lift off and up for a couple of feet, wheel, and come down for a quick landing before reinserting bill in ground. The neighbors two doors up the street in my small Virginia town provide another sort of meal for starlings; at precisely 8:20 every morning, they cast slices of white bread upon their neatly mowed back lawn. And, oh, the commotions! At least two dozen birds descend before the bread hits the grass. Left, right, left, right, they march briskly to the bread, grab it, and tug it apart, one bird to each corner of a slice. Then, like jugglers, they toss the tidbits in the air, catch them, toss again, prancing and leaping all the while, and when they finally tire of the game, either swallow or fly off with this fluffy white food they didn't work for. Later in the day, they may return for a more ordinary bout of probing for invertebrates in our neighbors' back yard.

But the starling could not have colonized—no, conquered—the country had it arrived on these shores with the earliest settlers, nor could it have gained so much as a clawhold for the next two or three centuries. The dense forests in the East, despite natural clearings, and the tallgrass prairies of the Great Plains gave little quarter to ground-feeding birds. It was ax and plough that created habitat suitable for the species. Or, to be less euphemistic, habitat was created by the people who set fires to clear away vegetation, who wielded tree-felling axes and grass-cutting scythes. Denuding the land, we made it starling-friendly. Nor is it likely that starlings would have settled in without some help. Though the European starling has ever been a migratory bird, breeding in Norway and Britain, for example, and wintering on Spain's Costa Brava, its seasonal movements cover limited territory. If it hadn't been for a man-made magic carpet, the Atlantic Ocean would have presented a daunting natural barrier to the species' westward expansion.

At this point, William Shakespeare figures in the tale. He is not, however, among those who have found the starling inspirational. Instead, he bids one of his characters to employ it as an instrument of mockery. The locus is *King Henry IV, Part I*. Henry considers Edmund Mortimer, the Earl of March, to be a traitor who gave up in battle and so "wilfully betray'd the lives of those he did lead to fight." He will not pay ransom for such a treasonous man. But the younger Henry Percy, known as Hotspur, protests, saying that Mortimer fought nobly, indeed was wounded, and suffered an honorable defeat. The king is not persuaded. Angered, frightened by the political threat that Mortimer poses, he enjoins Hotspur not to speak of Mortimer again. But immediately on Henry's departure from the scene, Hotspur tells his uncle, Thomas Percy, Earl of Worcester, that he shall speak to the king of Mortimer. And not only speak but find ingenious help in doing so. The indignant Hotspur tells his uncle that King Henry

> . . . said he would not ransom Mortimer;
> Forbade my tongue to speak of Mortimer;
> But I will find him when he lies asleep,
> And in his ear I'll holla 'Mortimer!'
> Nay, I'll have a starling shall be taught to speak
> Nothing but 'Mortimer,' and give it him,
> To keep his anger still in motion.

Here Shakespeare notes the starling's stellar gift for mimicry. And though the Bard does not say so outright, the bird that Hotspur intends to enlist as a torment to Henry will be a caged bird, one caught young, just fledged perhaps, and steadily tutored thereafter by regular repetition of the enraging word it is supposed to imitate.

"I knew I was the only person at the barn—my car was the only one in the parking lot," says Debra, who is married to my younger son. "When I went in, the horses nickered—this is normal. Then I thought I heard voices, multiple voices, and distinct snatches of speech just beyond my hearing comprehension. I actually walked through the barn and called out a couple of times. Even at midday, one doesn't want strangers hanging around a stable."

Because the study of art history does not yet provide Debra with much remuneration, she earns some money at a stable, exercising horses, grooming them, teaching riding, caring for tack, and just plain mucking out. The labor is not purely physical, however: she has also constructed the Heirloom Index, a genealogical data base for Egyptian Arabian horses of the stock owned by nineteenth-century pashas and khedives or collected in the desert, then bred in both Egypt and England, and exported all over the world by Lady Anne Blunt. But Debra's greatest benefit from the job is not the wages nor the satisfaction from having created a widely consulted data base, not to mention the glad chance to be outdoors in all seasons. Just as the children of a teacher in a private school often attend that school without fees, her own Egyptian Arabian, a stallion named Ibntep of Rose, is boarded there free of charge. Ibntep is a wonder horse, survivor of a broken leg, but that is another tale. He takes part in this story as the prime reason that Debra entered the barn that day: to ride him out and put him through all his elegant paces so that he could stretch his long silver-gray legs. But the voice of the impossible intruder gave her pause.

"The voices were still speaking when I returned to the door," she says. "I looked up then and saw a starling perched on a rafter, a single bird that continued to speak in human tongues as I watched and listened. Now and then it would punctuate its monologue with its own call and the calls of other birds. Starlings always remind me of those birdcall tapes and records—the sound is garbled and scratchy and skips from one song to another. But I was definitely hearing human phonemes."

As she stood there looking and listening, relieved that no one was rustling the animals or stealing tack, she wondered why the bird didn't imitate horses instead of people. Then she realized where this bird had learned its mumbles and its murmurations; she knew how it had picked up the sounds, if not the content, of human conversation. "Looking up at the bird reminded me of all the times I've driven down country roads and seen starlings lined up on the telephone wires. They tend to sit next to the poles when there are only a few birds, probably because there's less sway in the line. And that's where the leakage is greatest. I know a lineman who used to joke about all the things he heard when he rejoined phone lines."

So, among their many other failings, starlings are eaves-droppers.

At least once in history, starlings have been the models, not the imitators. My cousin Bess relates her own story, told to her by grown-ups after the event—and after they had realized that nothing ailed her. As a toddler, she spent most of her days and nights with a taciturn nursemaid on the third floor of a palatial stone house. Her bedroom lay under the eaves and overlooked a court-yard (I know that room; I've slept there, too). But despite her isolation from the rest of the household, she was a talkative child. The problem was, no one could understand her, for she spoke in whis-tles, screeches, and warbles. Worry spread upstairs and down that the child had a speech impediment or, worse, a deficient brain, and it persisted until the day that someone noticed the birds scrabbling, fussing, and probably nesting under the eaves. "A little kid repeats what it hears, and what I heard was bird," Bess says. "Of course I spoke starling."

In that respect then, starlings are like little kids, adept at repeating what they hear. And their stellar talent for mimicry was a subject for comment long before Shakespeare's time. The Roman naturalist Pliny the Elder, writing in the first century A.D., mentions a starling and several nightingales that belonged to Nero as a boy and to his stepbrother Britannicus, son of the emperor Claudius. The birds, given into the care of a trainer, were taught to utter words, then sentences of increasing length, in both Latin and Greek. Taking his feathered pupils into a quiet, private room, where no other sounds could interrupt and possibly influence the lessons, the trainer repeated words and rewarded success with food. Pliny remarks, as well, on other species that can be taught to talk—parrots, mag-pies—and declares that a magpie kept from repeating, repeating, repeating its favorite words will dwindle and die.

Pliny's record is one of the earliest to note the European starling's abilities as a vocal acrobat. (For ordinary, untutored starling-talk, the Romans used an onomatopoeic verb: *pisito*, I wheeze, I sigh, I hiss.) Pliny is far from the first, however, to make mention of the bird. In the Western tradition, Homer's *Iliad* may well have that honor, twice bringing an image of starlings—*psares* in Greek—into the fray of bat-tle and both times associating them with crows. In Book 16, the Greek warrior Patroclus, maddened by grief at the death of his best friend, strikes at the enemy's front lines like a hawk stooping at full speed to scatter frightened crows and starlings. In Book 17, the Tro-jans in turn relentlessly pursue the Greeks; Aeneas (who will sail west-ward after Troy's fall to found Rome) and the crown prince Hector charge the Greek army's rear, and the soldiers flee before them like a cloud of cawing, shrieking crows and starlings.

Starlings were rarer in Homer's day, and also in Shakespeare's, than they are at present. (The Bard is only waiting in the wings. He'll reenter after the story makes one or two more turns.) But whether starlings were more highly regarded in ages past than they are today, as a boon to some few, a bane to everybody else, is a question to which all the answers have been lost in the fogs of time. It is known, however, that the English word that designates the species is venerable indeed. The oldest English texts, dating back to the early 700s A.D., use the form *staer*. And the Lindesfarne Gospels, about A.D. 950, offer two *staras* instead of the canonical pair of sparrows in Matthew 10:29. Later, in the fifteenth century, *The Book of St. Albans*—treating of matters important to the nobility, like hawking, hunting, and heraldry—compiles and codifies venereal terms, particularly the group names that might (or might not) be important to hunters; here, familiar terms, like a school of fish and a host of angels, mingle with those that are decidedly inventive or outright strange, like a skulk of foxes and a husk of hares. The terms pertaining to birds show much imagination: a pitying of doves, a siege of herons, a murder of crows, a "murmuracion of stares." (It was definitely murmurations that Debra heard, not the sharper *pisito*.) In the early days, the suffix *-ling* was sometimes tacked on, sometimes left off (it may be a diminutive, though no one knows for certain, but it has since glued itself to the rest of the word, from which it is now inseparable). A Northumbrian poem of the fourteenth century sings of a sparrowhawk that flew by the "sterling," and a tale of King Arthur, written in the mid-1400s, brings in a battle image that might have come from Homer: "They smote in among them as a falcon among starlings." In 1667, the bird's gift for mimicry astonished Samuel Pepys, who wrote in his diary of a "starling which . . . do whistle and talk the most and best that ever I heard anything in my life." The bird's penchant for imitation continues to astound; in the 1980s, one Margarete Corbo wrote *Arnie, the Darling Starling* about her adventures with a garrulous bird, whom she found as a naked nestling and cared for fondly until its death four years later. She learned of its talent for mimicry when, one day, it suddenly shrieked the name she'd given it— "Arnie! Arnie!" But of her views, more later.

Mimicry: from all that's been said above, it may seem that the starling is confined to imitating talk, whistles, and telephone conversations, to Greek and Latin sentences or the endless hollering of "Mortimer." Not so: the bird's agile tongue finds stimulus in music, too. And so Mozart discovered to his amazement and delight. The place, Vienna; the year, 1784: soon after the composer had completed his Concerto for Piano and Orchestra in G Major (K. 453), he heard the happy little tune that informs the last movement played back to him out of the blue. Or rather, not out of the blue but out of the bill of a caged starling, which he bought immediately from a nearby shop for a sum that would amount to about twelve dollars in U.S. currency today. In this case, composer inspired starling; the bird had listened well while the man had fingered the piano keys and put the piece together. A surviving description notes, however, that the bird's mimicry was not perfect, for it sang a G sharp instead of the G flat that had been written into the music. Mozart, enchanted, forgiving the bird, commented, "That was lovely." Not much later, in 1787, the roles were reversed: starling inspired composer. The man also knew how to listen well and, using what he'd heard, wrote a sextet for strings and two horns that one critic has described this way: "Full of wrong notes, structural defects, uncalled for cadenzas, the piece represents a playful, practical-joking vein in Mozart of which his biography gives ample evidence, but which his music seldom exhibits." The critic does not mention Mozart's pet, but here there is no doubt that the music imitates the bird. Throughout, the notes are embellished with murmurs, wheezes, whistles, and sighs, and the very last note is a loud, ungainly, completely appropriate squawk. The piece (K. 522) has been nicknamed *ein musikalischer Spass*, a musical joke. And what a merry jest it is!

In 1880, less than a century later, Cassell's *Natural History* delivered a pronouncement that all too soon came to seem like a joke: "The Starlings are found only in the Old World, where they form a very large and natural Group."

Reenter Shakespeare, the man behind the man who provided European starlings with their magic carpet. In 1890 and 1891, only a flash of time after Cassell had made his definitive assignment of starlings to the Old World, flocks totalling eighty to a hundred birds altogether were brought across the Atlantic and released in New York City's Central Park. The importer was Eugene Scheiffelin, the leading light of an acclimatization society. Such societies, with the laudable aim of aiding and abetting the exchange of plants and animals from one part of the world to another, were founded by the dozens in the nineteenth century. In the case of starlings, this aim was realized with measureless success. Scheiffelin's starlings were not the first, however, to have been brought westward. Earlier attempts had been made at settling the species in the New World, notably in California, where a small flock languished for several years in the 1880s before it disappeared. What the motive for that particular introduction might have been, I do not know. But the reason for Scheiffelin's importation has lasted as stubbornly as the birds that he released in Central Park: Shakespeare. In an admiring, entirely well-meant obeisance to the playwright's memory, he planned to bring to the United States every avian species that Shakespeare mentioned. And birds certainly inhabit the plays and poems—birds like the thrush, jay, and lark of *The Winter's Tale;* the sweet-singing nightingales and wrens of several venues; and, in *Macbeth,* the darkly ominous "maggot-pies and choughs and rooks." One hallowed Shakespearean species—the tiny wren that we know as the winter wren—was native to North America as well as to Europe; another—chanticleer, the rooster, along with his hens—had been most successfully imported and established by the Spaniards who explored all the Americas decades before Shakespeare set pen to paper and centuries before Scheiffelin thought to honor the Bard. But where today are the New World's nightingales, and where our song thrushes, skylarks, and crowlike choughs? The only introduced Shakespearean species that have taken hold are the starling and the house sparrow (Scheiffelin brought in the house sparrow, too, but he was only one of many sponsors of that most successful immigrant). And the starling has not just taken hold but taken as its rightful fiefdom more territory than anyone could have foretold.

The timeline for success reads this way: 1890, release in Central Park. 1920, a sure claim staked out to the mid-Atlantic states along the eastern side of the Appalachians, from Chesapeake Bay down through the Carolinas. 1930, except for Maine, occupation of the United States west to—and sometimes across—the mighty Mississippi. 1940, Maine taken over, along with much of New Brunswick; the birds' western limit now marked by the Rockies, with incursions into Mexico and Manitoba. 1950, another push west, this time to California's coast range, and another push north, into the southernmost regions of British Columbia. 1960, a large new claim established, from the southern tip of Canada's Georgian Bay west to the Pacific, thence south to Baja California. And still no end to the great grab: land seized in the Northwest Territories and Alaska, some of it at latitudes above the Arctic Circle. By 1993, a modest count numbered the offspring of the hundred birds released by Scheiffelin at a quite immodest two hundred million.

A simple formula describes the birds' explosive expansion in a single century: starlings increase in number with a growth in the human population. As we develop places for ourselves to live, the starlings see an open invitation and move right in. Symbiosis—that's the proper word to denominate the unwitting interaction between *Homo sapiens* and *S. vulgaris,* and its form is commensalism, in which one species gains but the other receives nothing whatsoever, no reward and no penalty. And in the involuntary arrangement between starlingkind and humanity, another element comes into play: try though we do, we can't shake off the association. Wherever we go, the starling follows. The only places in the continental United States in which the bird is uncommon are exactly those places that discourage us—the stony, treeless peaks and ridges of the Rockies, the sere landscapes of northern New Mexico, and Alaska's high tundra.

But commensalism accounts for only some of the starling's success. The bird has inner resources to call on: an almost omnivorous appetite, an eye for the advantage, a flair for adapting instanter to changing circumstances, a profound wariness, and a hair-trigger instinct for self-preservation. I'm also confident that the bird possesses an intellect greater than that found within most feathered skulls. But it's the appetite that most amazes me. Or rather, the anatomical acrobatics that allow the starling to alter its dining habits according to seasonal rhythms in the abundance or scarcity of certain foods. The facts about this biological feat first came to my attention through the 1993 booklet *European Starling*, Number 48 in the series of monographs issued on North American birds by the American Ornithologists' Union. In the warmer months, *S. vulgaris* dines mainly on a grand cafeteria of insects, along with other invertebrates like snails, earthworms, and spiders. When cold weather sets in and insect life huddles quiescently in winter quarters, plants provide the bird's primary diet; the list of preferred items includes both wild and domesticated fruits—plums, cherries, holly and sumac berries, hackberries, the applelike fruit of hawthorns, the small blue-black drupes of the black gum. But vegetables are harder than meat for a bird to digest. Since aboriginal times, however, the starling's gut has taken that inconvenience into account. During the frigid months, not only does the gizzard grow larger, but the gut also lengthens, and so do the villi—the tiny, hairlike intestinal protuberances that help absorb nutriments. And vegetables speed through the bird's gut at a clip far faster than that of meat.

But my greatest reward for latching on to Number 48 in the AOU's series has lain not so much in acquiring such arcane snippets of starling lore as in talking with Paul Cabe, the scientist who wrote it. And getting together with him to talk about starlings was yet another example of what I've come to think of as the small-world phenomenon, which is the oddly recurrent concatenation of the past with the present, the wonderfully unexpected awakening of dormant connections. When I ordered the monograph from a specialist in ornithological books, I was unaware of my earlier acquaintance with its author. But my memory was jostled by his familiar surname and, more, by his mention of collecting starlings in the Virginia county where I spend each winter. I'd first met Paul a good fifteen years before reading his work, had met him indeed when he was just a boy, not a slender, bearded man with a splendidly shaggy, home-barbered mop of chestnut-brown hair. He's now halfway through his fourth decade and teaches courses in biology and environmental studies at Saint Olaf College in Northfield, Minnesota. His parents—running a local business, performing frequently in summer theater and winter play-readings, restoring a quirkily Victorian house in the small town of my growing up—have forever been part of my days. One of his sisters is also a leading light of the county's bird club. Back home during his Christmas break, Paul sits at my kitchen table munching on a sandwich and answering a flock of questions between bites. With him is his slim, sloe-eyed and dark-haired, very pretty wife, Leigh Ann Beavers, who is an ardent starling partisan in her own right. She calls them "one of the prettiest birds we have."

"Yes, but," says Paul, "starlings are like certain kinds of music, loud and raucous, very hard to listen to."

"Yes, but," Leigh Ann responds, "there are melodies underneath."

Paul is by trade a population geneticist, not an ornithologist. And it is he around whom a suspicion of witchcraft crystalized. The factual basis for this canard may be found in his choice, years before, of a subject for his dissertation, which investigated starling populations in different areas of the United States, comparing them and seeking to uncover genetic variations from group to group. Why starlings? Because of their abundance and ubiquity, they'd be easy to collect for the samples needed, and, yes, he had obtained the permits necessary for legally taking birds, even those of the pestiferous sort. He hoped to "find signatures on a geographic scale that showed how they expanded across North America." And given a mere hundred ancestors for the millions on tens of millions of birds now peppering the New World, it seemed possible that the species might show evidence of population bottlenecks. A bottleneck occurs when the gene pool available to a species as a whole becomes limited because a founding group is small or a residual population, like that of the black-footed ferret or the Florida panther, is tiny. These isolated groups do not have access to genetic variety. In Paul's estimation, however, "One hundred individuals is not a small bottleneck." Sufficient variety was imported with the birds. Yet they themselves had the potential for creating new bottlenecks as small flocks with little variation in their genes migrated hither and yon, not so gradually spreading from the Atlantic to the Pacific. Starlings like to move; they migrate readily, with flocks that swell, diminish, then swell again as birds come and go. Checking on possible differences among populations, looking for signatures, Paul collected birds in Virginia, Vermont, Colorado, and California. Mathematical predictions of what should have happened turned out to be predictions of what had actually happened: the New World's birds showed only an insignificant decrease in genetic variation. Had geographic expansion left a signature in current populations? Apparently not; his work suggested that any differences so created would be ephemeral, for each population of European starlings in the United States is much the same as any other. While birds like fox sparrows that stay put and live in geographic islands, one in this valley, another in the next, show high degrees of difference—high, that is, compared to other kinds of birds— among their separate communities, only a low degree pertains among birds that are quick to travel. Paul says, "Starlings move around so much that any differences there might have been are erased."

It was en route to these conclusions that Paul found himself suspected of involvement in diabolic rites. For his studies of genetic differences among starlings, he took tissue samples from dead birds and stored them in liquid nitrogen till testing time. The testing procedure that he used was molecular—"a fairly old, late-sixties technique"—that looks at particular enzymes and examines the differences in the DNA-directed structures of their proteins. One balmy afternoon Paul decided to pursue his tissue-taking labors on the back porch of the Victorian house that his parents had barely begun to renovate. As his father, Tom Cabe, describes it, the dwelling was nothing more than a "tumbledown, haunted wreck, surrounded by ailanthus trees and overgrown boxwood," and the family was living in the nearby carriage house, actually a garage with a second-floor apartment that had been built on the foundations of a nineteenth-century stable. The porch was a better locale, airier and brighter, for the task of dissecting starlings. The scene that met the eyes of a child exploring the neighborhood and peeking through the boxwood was that of a grown man working with the fiercest, most minutely focused attention on—oh, no!—dead birds. And not just dead but black! Horror-struck, the child-spy ran back to the aunt she was visiting and babbled that she'd seen a bearded man doing rituals behind the Cabes' house. But what else could she have thought at the sight of someone picking apart those little, dark-as-midnight carcasses?

Alive, the birds are beautiful. Leigh Ann and I agree on that. Their old feathers shine glossy black, with a faint iridescence like that of oil shimmering on dark water. (According to Debra, my art-historian daughter-in-law, birds see more of the color spectrum than people do, and so the iridescence must appear to them as a "brilliant, dazzling array of moving color.") And their new feathers, donned after the yearly summertime molt, are decorated with delicate, lacy white spots. For the spring breeding season, the dark gray-brown bills of all the adults, male and female, turn to a rich golden yellow. And their legs—always eager to strut and march, prance and cavort—are cinnamon-brown.

"Each bird is an individual," Leigh Ann says. "If you see them perched on a wire, each one is doing something different—preening, stretching its wings, lifting its bill, whistling, taking a nap. No two are alike."

This view of starlings is one for which the Minnesota State Arts Board has awarded her a grant. She is a printmaker, working mainly with intaglio monotypes. To achieve them, she uses various methods to incise Plexiglas and copper plates with lines into which ink is forced; the tops of the plates are then wiped clean and run with paper through a press. Sometimes she enhances the images formed by the lines with monoprinting, a technique that adds ink to the surface of the plate in order to create complexities of shading and tone. Her recently funded project celebrates the starlings introduced to Central Park by Eugene Scheiffelin a little more than a century ago. Eighty birds? One hundred? Because no one knows exactly how many were released, Leigh Ann has settled on a happy medium of ninety, with each portrayed in a way unlike that of its eighty-nine companions. The time-consuming preliminary task of photographing starlings doing almost everything they can do has been painstakingly accomplished. The fine limited-edition intaglios have been made. And Leigh Ann has had a sponsored show of ninety starlings in ninety different modes of display.

Little did Scheiffelin know what he had wrought for the world of art when he imported stocky black birds with raucous voices and antic habits. Not just the visual but also the verbal arts have benefited from his act of homage. Not that starlings haven't been noticed immemorially by poets, and in our time, they have furnished W. H. Auden with a tender and hopeful simile. In the prologue to "On This Island," he offers a prayer to Love and asks that longing bring a man's thought "Alive like patterns a murmuration of starlings,/Rising in joy over wolds, unwittingly weave." "Joy" seems the meet word to describe the instinctive speed and synchronicity with which a large flock lifts and wheels, but Auden's starlings rise over the rolling, open uplands of his native England. It is John Updike who has noticed descendants of Scheiffelin's birds and proceeded not only to sing them but to let them name his poem "The Great Scarf of Birds."

The place is a golf course, in Updike's Ipswich I would think, for it lies on the edge of a salt marsh. The time is autumn, leaves turning orange and red, the geese flying south. The "trumpeting" of geese induces the poet and his golfing companions to look upward. And they see this:

> As if out of the Bible
> or science fiction,
> a cloud appeared, a cloud of dots
> like iron filings which a magnet
> underneath the paper undulates.
> It dartingly darkened in spots,
> paled, pulsed, compressed, distended, yet
> held an identity firm: a flock
> of starlings, as much one thing as a rock.
> One will moved above the trees
> the liquid and hesitant drift.

The starlings landed and thickly covered the grass of the fairway. But as the poet watched, one bird rose. Instantly,

> . . . lifting in a casual billow,
> the flock ascended as a lady's scarf,
> transparent, of gray, might be twitched
> by one corner, drawn upward, and then,
> decided against, negligently tossed toward a chair:
> dissolving all anxiety,
> the southward cloud withdrew into the air.

It does not diminish this poem as art to say that it is also an act of science: its description of starling behavior shows an acuity that might be envied by any naturalist.

"What good are starlings?" I ask Paul Cabe. "Or, to put it otherwise, how bad are they?"

He admits that they can be pests. At least, they're seen as such, notably in urban settings. And, showing a special fondness for cherries, they can strip orchards bare. As for their effect on other birds, he says, "Starlings probably depress the population densities of medium-sized woodpeckers and other cavity-nesting species. The great crested flycatchers are hard hit. But starlings won't drive any bird to extinction."

Nor will starlings come to cause more widespread ruination than they do now, with every orchard failing, every city thickly, hopelessly mired in droppings. The general despicability of starlings seems to me largely a matter of perception. How to improve their public image? How to turn each one into a "darling starling," like the garrulous Arnie? That bird's keeper, Margarete Corbo, obligingly provides us with a theory: "Since we never consider as a nuisance those creatures with whom we choose to share our lives, my solution would be known as Adopt a Starling." She adds that we should cease trying to rid ourselves of Arnie's brethren in favor of giving all bird lovers starlings that "shall be taught to speak nothing but 'Mortimer.'" Alas, despite its brave support for this most unpopular of birds, the theory lacks all practicality.

It occurs to me then to ask Paul a subversive question, a question that pushes the bounds of ecological correctness: "Suppose, just suppose that the cosmic plug were somehow pulled and all European starlings went the way of the dodo. Are starlings necessary?"

Paul replies, "I think about this sort of question a lot. It comes up frequently in environmental studies and conservation biology. My opinion is that for most species, extinction will not have cata-

strophic community or ecosystem results. Other species will probably shift their abundance, but nothing will disappear or fall apart."

And what might a world without starlings be like? A world
without starlings probing the soil of pastures, golf courses, and the
median strips of four-lane highways? Without starlings listening to
conversations through the high wires along every street and country
lane? Without starlings not just barging into woodpecker holes and
bird boxes but also invading attics, eaves, and clothes-dryer vents to
build their nests? Without starlings marching, prancing, and fighting
over bread or lifting into air as lightly as a lady's scarf?

"I think we would have fewer urban birds," Paul says. "I have
never been able to think of any native species which would do as
well in cities."

February: once again, winter recedes. The starlings shine glossy
black, and their yellow bills advertise the advent of the breeding
season. My annual sojourn in the valley of Virginia is nearly done;
I'll soon head back to North Carolina's wide and salty river Neuse.
There in the woodpeckers' condo-tree, I'll see another round of
winner-takes-all. No sense making book on the winner's identity. But
the red-bellied woodpeckers, the great crested flycatchers, the
pushed-aside others have grand instincts for beating the odds.
They'll be calling, nesting, and replicating themselves this year, next
year, and in years to come.

And another question, quite unlooked for, surfaces: What if the
cosmic plug were pulled on us? Is *Homo sapiens* necessary?

I'm willing to bet that if we weren't around, clearing land and
raising cities, there'd be fewer starlings.

But it's my daughter-in-law Debra who has the last word. In
addition to horses she takes care of small animals, particularly those
that have suffered injury or abandonment. Her skills were long ago
gained by rearing starlings and pigeons that had fallen from their
nests. So starlings are old acquaintances. "I've felt a smile creep over
my face," she writes, "listening to a starling go through its scratchy

repertoire of songs, and I honed my bird-listening ear figuring out which species it was imitating."

It's her ornithomorphism—her ability to see humankind in the image of a bird—that most catches my attention. She calls starlings the "clowns" of the bird world and its "gaudy gypsies, with voices pretending to be many of their neighbors." And she adds, "They are raucous, rude, wildly adaptable, murderous, thieving, irreverent mockers. Are they birds or humans? All of us have a little starling inside us, some more than others."

Amen.

THE NATURAL HISTORY OF PROTEUS

Small Lobose Amoeba

Scaled Cyst Stage

Zoospore

Filose Amoeba

Stage with Extended Flagellum

Large Lobose Amoeba

Pfiesteria piscicida

NORTH Carolina's wide and salty river Neuse flows seventy-five feet from my front door. For fourteen years I've watched it, for fourteen summers set my crab pots and pulled a gill net out from the riverbank. At times, many of the menhaden in the net would show oozing red sores in the anal area, and some of the crab shells would be deeply pitted, as if they'd been burned with a red-hot poker. I kept the fish as bait for the pots but tossed back damaged crabs. The trouble, however, was occasional, with a low incidence of apparent disease. Then, in September 1995, I saw a strange glint on the river—sunlight reflected off a thousand thousand floating, bobbing silver carcasses. The water close inshore was covered with dead fish.

Fish kills have occurred for many reasons since fish first came to swim, hundreds of millions of years ago, in the waters of the world. But only in the last decade has it been recognized that the sores, the deformities, the dying may signal the presence of a shape-changer. As infinitely agile as Proteus, the Old Man of the Sea, it lives, feasts, and replicates itself beneath the surface of the waves. And at one and the same time, like Proteus, it is powerful, dangerous, prophetic.

Homer has given us the mythic history of that ancient Proteus, and the old Greek tale has once again found new life in English. Feisty and eloquent, in lines that surge like a swelling, lapsing sea, it is recounted in Robert Fagles's recent version of *The Odyssey*. The venue for the story is the salty deeps of the Mediterranean and Pharos, the island located a hard day's sail from the Egyptian coast. There, the Old Man of the Sea regularly comes ashore with his retinue of seals and curls up in a cave to sleep away the sea-washed afternoons. And there, Menelaus has been marooned for twenty days. After leaving the smoke-blackened ruins of Troy and pausing in Egypt on his way back to Sparta, he has come this far only to find that heaven is holding back the winds. Sails limp, rations nearly gone, stamina running low, he and his crew have almost lost hope for a day of safe return. Then one of the god's daughters offers help.

Ambush Proteus, she says, catch the "immortal Old Man of the Sea who never lies"; he will instruct you how to cross the "swarming sea" and reach the shores of home. And she gives Menelaus a warning to

> muster your heart and hold him fast,
> wildly as he writhes and fights you to escape.
> He'll try all kinds of escape—twist and turn
> into every beast that moves across the earth,
> transforming himself into water, superhuman fire,
> but you hold on for dear life, hug him all the harder!

Proteus does just that: he shifts—*zip*—with pelting, dazing speed from god into lion, serpent, panther, wild boar, torrential cataract, towering tree, and back to god again. Parting at last with the information Menelaus longs for, how to call forth the necessary, sail-filling winds and set course again, the Old Man of the Sea also prophesies the past, present, and future of the other Greeks who fought at Troy. And more, he tells Menelaus precisely what act of hybris so angered the gods that they stranded him on Pharos: in his haste to go home, the lord of Sparta had failed to make the proper sacrifices before he embarked from Egypt. He will, however, be given a chance to retrace his route and make amends.

Split-second transformations, resounding prophecy, a warning against arrogance: these are the main elements in the mythic history of Proteus. They are present also in the natural history of the shape-changer that ranges the creeks, estuaries, and sounds of our coast from the Chesapeake Bay to the southern tip of Florida. With striped bass, bluefish, and blue crabs, with speckled trout and sea horses, these waters swarm as actively as the Homeric sea. (They host bottle-nosed dolphins, too, the very species that escorted the Greek ships across the Aegean sea to Troy.) And the Proteus within the deeps and shallows here, though older than the idea of time, rose only an instant ago into human ken. First reported in 1985, it was identified in the early 1990s by JoAnn Burkholder, an aquatic botanist at North Carolina State University, as a dinoflagellate, a microscopic organism and one unlike any that had ever before swum into our awareness. A marine creature, it seems to prefer brackish and saline habitats, though it has been known to range off-shore in the full-strength salt of the Atlantic ocean. Some scientists believe that, in any of its habitats, it may assume as many as twenty-four fluent shapes during its life cycle; others opt for a maximum of eight. The precise number of stages is not so important, however, as the fact that some of them are toxic, killing fish as surely as the dynamite still used by a few scofflaw fishermen.

The discovery of this protean dinoflagellate and its predatory habits have been widely noted by the media: TV news reports and documentaries; National Public Radio commentaries; articles in magazines as various as *Outdoor Life, U.S. News & World Report,* and *Sports Illustrated;* and, not least, a 364-page book ominously entitled *When the Waters Turned to Blood.* Written by Rodney Barker, published in 1997, it sensationalizes politics and personalities but scants the creature's natural history. The author also offers considerable misin-formation. The title, for example, implies that the presence of the dinoflagellate in an active state is signaled when our sounds and rivers turn red. No; the phenomenon known as a "red tide" is due entirely to other microorganisms. And he writes that the word *dinoflagellate* is pronounced with a short *i.* Not so; the *i* is long, as in *dire.* The most egregious error lurks in his statement that the organ-ism belongs not to the plant kingdom but to that of the animals. In reality, it inhabits neither. Biologists, though they bicker about the precise number, have added three or four more kingdoms to the list. Joining the classic duumvirate of Plantae and Animalia are the Prokaryotes (sometimes called the Monera), single-celled organisms that lack a nucleus; the Protista, single-celled and other microscopic organisms with a nucleus; and the Fungi, from shiitakes and chanterelles to the causative agents of athlete's foot. With all other dinoflagellates, the Proteus in our sounds, estuaries, and brackish creeks dwells amid the Protista, the "very first ones," a kingdom in which diatoms, simple algae, and the slime molds also hold sway. It's a kingdom far more primal than those of plants and animals.

This creature nearly as old as the sea has been formally named *Pfiesteria piscicida* (pronounced Feast-EAR-ee-ah pis-kih-SEED-ah). The genus, which was assigned by Dr. Burkholder, honors the late Lois Pfiester (1936–1992), an algal biologist who specialized in freshwater dinoflagellates. Dr. Burkholder's original choice for the species name, *piscimortis* or "fish death," was invalidated by the rules of scientific nomenclature, and Karen Steinhalter of the University of Florida came up with the far more vigorous descriptive term *piscicida*, which translates into "fish killer." At least two species of *Pfiesteria*, including *piscicida*, have been identified in the coastal rivers of North Carolina, and two more in the Chesapeake Bay and its tributaries.

Dinoflagellate, an ecumenical word that combines the Greek *dinos* with the Latin *flagella*, means "whirling whips" and describes the threadlike filaments, usually two, that the organisms use to propel themselves up, down, and sideways through the water. Many species are protected by an outer membrane of cellulose called a theca; others, only thinly covered, are termed "naked" or "unarmored" dinoflagellates. Fish killer, an armored species, takes the standard form in several of its incarnations. Then—*zip*—it changes. The typically ovoid, daintily flagellated single cell becomes larger and assumes the shape of an amoeba with arms like the points of stars. *Zip*—it loses definition and spreads into an even larger amoeba, flattened and lobed. *Zip*—this stage turns itself into a minuscule spore that drifts in the water or into a ball-like cyst that sinks to the bottom and waits. Nor is shifting into these shapes and a slew of others the only way in which fish killer exhibits a stunning virtuosity. Sometimes it eats flesh; sometimes, like a plant, it feeds itself by photosynthesis. The latter is accomplished through a kind of swift, silent mugging: fish killer is a specialized thief—a kleptochloroplast, in formal terms—that steals chlorophyll from its rightful owners. In some incarnations it may be toxic; in others, benign. It is equally artful, equally devious in matters of reproduction, able to perpetuate its own kind either by sexual means or vegetatively through cell division. There is no set order for any of these changes. Fish killer spins through myriad transformations in accord with the varying signals delivered by its environment. It is, for example, the natural secreta—the flaking tissues, the excrement—of passing schools of fish that trigger a carnivorous frenzy. *Zip*—with a sudden twist, this microscopic ambush-predator changes from sleeping cyst to star or flattened sphere and releases a toxin that makes fish lethargic and injures their skin so that they are no longer able to maintain their internal salt balance. Open, sometimes hemorrhaging lesions may develop. The tiny predator feeds then on the blood and sloughed tissues. And when the fish die, fish killer reverts to a benign phase and feeds on the carcasses.

Fish killer's quick changes, its multiple disguises are not unique among dinoflagellates; some freshwater species have been observed to have as many as three dozen life stages. Though its style of predation seems extraordinary, other *Pfiesteria*-like dinoflagellates almost certainly employ similar techniques. And the creature's general noxiousness is shared by a sizable group of Protista. These species are known collectively as harmful algal blooms, a term that's been condensed into an easy-to-pronounce acronym, HAB. Several varieties of HAB cause the notorious red tides that occur in coastal waters. Not all red tides bloom red; some may be brown or yellow-green. But no matter the color, every one is the work of a species of dinoflagellate, like *Gonyaulax polyedra*, *G. catenella*, or the unarmored *Gymnodium breve*. Many of these dinoflagellates contain potent neurotoxins. Clams, oysters, and scallops that feed on them are able to store the toxins in their flesh without ill effect, but should a fish swim through contaminated waters, it will suffer paralysis and die. Should a human being eat shellfish harvested from tainted waters, or even breathe red-tidal surf or spray flung into the air, the central nervous system will be attacked: sickness, paralysis, sometimes death. It's *G. breve*—the "naked, short" species—that flouted the common belief that red tides occur only in sultry summer: riding the Gulf Stream, it swept up the North Carolina coast from Florida in

October 1987, and persisted till the end of December. Coastal waters were closed to shellfishing; trawlers and dredges stayed in harbor; seafood markets shut their doors. Since then, the red tides of the Southeastern coast have kept themselves elsewhere—off Texas and Florida, for example—but nothing guarantees that these lethally colorful HAB species will never return to the Carolinas and the river Neuse. Another sort of HAB, probably a dinoflagellate (though it may be a diatom, with a siliceous skeleton) is believed to be the cause of ciguatera, or tropical fish poisoning. Fish like dog snappers and some species of amberjack eat smaller fish that have fed on this toxin-producing protist, and people who innocently dine upon affected food-fish suffer serious consequences to the central nervous system.

It is speculated that *P. piscicida* may also inflict harm on human beings. Nausea, loss of memory, lesions on the skin—these and other possible effects have been reported. Cause and effect, however, have not been firmly linked, nor have fish killer's particular toxins been identified. But tutored by my own experience, I can firmly state this much: cuts from sharp fish scales and puncture wounds from the spines of fish and crabs are as septic as a dog's bite or that of a man. It's likely that many—not all, but many—of the infections blamed on fish killer are triggered instead by failure to cleanse the wounds and apply antiseptics. I suspect, too, that the human propensity to place blame elsewhere thrusts fish killer into the role of a scapegoat. Nonetheless, if someone should fall into water that abounds with dead fish, these are the recommendations: bathe as soon as possible, washing off with soap and uncontaminated water or a solution of one part household bleach to ten parts water.

What is fish killer's role in the world? Much has been said about the interdependence of all the great and small lives on earth. On the Carolina coast, I see the concept illustrated by myriad symbiotic relationships: the yucca fertilized by a specially adapted moth; the isopod that lives in the mouth of a menhaden and uses its

host as a food-catching device; the aquatic grasses that serve as
nurseries for new-hatched mullet and red drum, as food for mallards
and canvasbacks; the black tupelos that entice migrating birds with
their high-energy fruit and are then rewarded by avian dispersal of
the seeds. In these relationships, at least one party needs the other
to survive. The common metaphor is the "web of life"; the picture is
that of intricate, often messy interconnections—a sticky fabric spun
all higgledy-piggledy by a drunken spider—in which anything
affecting one strand reverberates through all the others. Damage
leads to the endangerment of living species, breaks mean their
extinction, and all of us—moths, isopods, fish, plants, birds, people—are the poorer for destruction of any part of the web. But how
does this conventional view of the natural scheme accommodate the
nefarious HAB species? What is their place in the tanglement of
things? What can their purpose possibly be?

P. piscicida and its kin are opportunists. They have a place on
the low end of the food chain, yes, and in the lab, fish killer has
been seen to serve as supper for slightly larger aquatic organisms,
like rotifers and copepods (not to mention the journalists of the late
1990s who have feasted gluttonously on its newly recognized presence). No other life-form, however, is dependent on fish killer for its
own survival. The ecological role of any HAB may best be understood if it is viewed as an organism subtly, ingeniously adapted to
take advantage of its habitat. Like the European starling that long
ago seized the chance to exploit a subterranean larder of grubs and
worms not accessible to other birds, like the kudzu vine that grows
in soils too poor in nutrients to support other vegetation, the HAB
species have made themselves at home in niches that are otherwise
unoccupied or underused. Indeed, with one huge exception, all
earth's living entities, both great and small, are niche dwellers. The
exception, of course, is we the people, who scrambled out of our
original hunting-gathering niche only a brief ten to twelve thousand
years ago when we managed to domesticate our plant and animal
food. Since then, we've been roaming ever farther afield, exploring

the planet, flying to the moon, and en route discovering a few creatures that are something like ourselves and teeming multitudes that
are not. The first category is filled primarily with mammals and marsupials; the second with aliens, some of which, like goldfish and
ladybugs, are humanly acceptable, while others, like rattlesnakes,
ticks, tapeworms, and P. piscicida, are only to be cussed, avoided, and
killed when possible. The aliens are numerous and wily, and they
know their niches far better than we do.

But why should the HAB species in general and P. piscicida in
particular—these aboriginal protists that have swarmed almost forever in this planet's waters—seem to have become newly malevolent? Or not malevolent, for they are not capable of forming wishes,
but rather explosively predatory where once they'd seemed quiet
and well behaved?

Considering these questions, I am reminded of the sea changes
that the passage of millennia has worked in the Nereids. According
to classical myth, these saltwater nymphs, daughters of the sea god
Nereus, sported with Poseidon and Proteus in the waters of the fish-
friendly sea. Riding bow waves along with the dolphins, they
escorted Achilles' ships to Troy. And I like to think that as they gam-
boled in the surf and swelling combers, the sea glowed not just with
phosphorescence but with the playful holiness of their presence.
Between those times and ours, however, the position of the Nereids
in Greek folk belief has been altered. They are no longer seen as
bright, good-natured spirits but have assumed a dark, demonic character. A friend tells me that on the island of Rhodes he met an old
man who said he'd encountered the Nereids one night. How did he
respond? "I drew a cross on the ground and a circle around it," he
told my friend, "and I stayed in the circle till dawn." Precisely why
the Nereids' luster has been extinguished, my friend did not say.

Like the daughters of Nereus, fish killer has lived in the world's
waters well-nigh onto forever. And like those sea nymphs it has
become an object of fear. Though it has always fed itself by stealing
chloroplasts to enable photosynthesis or by engaging in chemical

warfare to acquire meat, its populations now burgeon, becoming more ravenous and lethal every day. What accounts for this great burst of insatiability?

Enter prophecy. The Greeks knew that it might be used not just to predict the future but also to tell the truth about the present. The Proteus in our streams and sounds, captured at last and identified, delivers a twofold truth. Its first component is the nutrient overload—the pollution—in coastal waters. Corn and soy farms, hog and poultry operations, pulp mills and phosphate mines, military-aircraft-repair depots, towns with water-treatment plants, rural waterfront communities with septic systems, the weedless and chemically lush riverfront lawn of my neighbor three doors down— all these and more variously release fertilizers, heavy metals, animal and human wastes, and other unnatural ingredients into the water. The bottoms where fish killer is wont to hide till prey comes swimming by are also paved with new detritus, from dead algae to mud washed down the river from raw residential developments under construction two hundred miles upstream. Like a tonic, like the kiss of a prince, this broth—particularly rich in phosphorus and nitrogen compounds—has waked the organism from its slumber. *P. piscicida* has always caused fish kills, but now, at century's end, its lethal work is seen with increasing frequency.

The second part of fish killer's truth is that of the increased stratification of its aqueous habitat. In the summer, when the dinoflagellate is most predaceous, the water in estuaries becomes layered: freshwater from rain and runoff flowing downstream meets wedges of denser saltwater working their way upstream, and the two pile up, one over the other, rather than mingling. This phenomenon is natural. The problem is that it's being unnaturally intensified, and in two ways. First, factors like farming, urban paving, and growing development of the watershed lead to a great increase in runoff (and to the likelihood of floods, especially in times of nor'easter or hurricane). Then, with private and commercial development and the consequent removal of vegetation and with the steady loss of wetlands, there has been a concomitant decrease in the ability of the soil to soak up water and release it slowly. When rain and runoff cannot be stored, they enter the water in all-or-nothing spurts. And when the summertime flow downstream is robbed of freshwater because none has been held back for steady release, then saltwater intrudes with greater force. But come a storm and a burst of heavy runoff, the flow of freshwater will also be enhanced. And when large amounts of freshwater become layered with large amounts of salt, fish killer especially rejoices.

Yet a third element in fish killer's transformation from peaceable microbe to terrorist was posited in 1997 by a physician working with river-related illnesses in coastal Maryland. He made the logical speculation that copper is implicated. Copper, added to animal feeds to prevent spoilage, forms salts when it is leached from manure piles, particularly on factory farms producing hogs and poultry. With other agricultural runoff, the salts then enter waterways, where they kill the algae and cryptomonads on which the dinoflagellate feeds in its benign state. Then, cupboard bare of its customary food, it must look for other prey.

Clearly, we've made the life of *P. piscicida* far easier by offering it an increased supply of food and better furnishings for the niche it's filled since time out of mind. And with these new comforts, the organism's noxiousness has been exacerbated. Its populations explode. Dead fish—menhaden, flounder, croaker, spot, a host of others—rise and float on the surface in great rafts. Battening on their flesh, fish killer ceases to reproduce vegetatively and becomes a sexual creature. But when it is sated or disturbed, it encysts itself, sinks to the soft bottom, and once again waits.

The Proteus of estuaries and sounds has given warning: we have been as neglectful as Menelaus of our responsibilities. We have not given due respect to nature's invisible forces. And our particular hybris has consisted of making heedless assumptions about water's ability to flush away chemical insults.

But the glare of nationwide publicity has at last, after more than a decade of denial and foot dragging, embarrassed the government of North Carolina, where fish killer's toxic work has been most evident, into setting up clean-water standards and authorizing funds to monitor the rivers and sounds and reduce their burden of pollution. Maryland and Virginia, where either fish killer or a closely related dinoflagellate has only recently been discovered, have been far less sluggardly; they sprang instantly into action, closing the streams in which it was found to both commercial fishing and recreation. Those waters have since been reopened but will be closed again should fish killer reappear in lethal form.

The moral is that where there's evidence pointing to fish killer's presence, the most useful approach is that of exercising caution and common sense. Here on the wide and salty Neuse, when the water flows free of floating carcasses and the shells of the blue crabs are clean, my neighbors and I are safe in setting crab pots and pulling out our nets. To our good fortune, such benignity is the river's customary mode.

As species, *P. piscicida* and the others in its genus are well-nigh immortal. Try as we will, our best efforts can in no way cause their endangerment, much less push them into extinction. And should some eruption of chance, some unimaginable accident, exterminate the creatures but leave all other life on earth intact, other equally hungry opportunists would move into the vacant niche. We do, however, have the power to damp fish killer's appetites, to reduce its ravages. Like Menelaus, we still have a chance to clean up our own act and make amends.

Planozygote

BLOOD

Black Horsefly (*Tabanus atratus*)

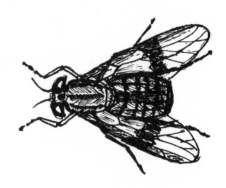

Deerfly (*Chrysops vittatus*)

The Tabanids—Deerflies and Horseflies

I N mid-May, beware. Stay clear of coastal Carolina's deep green
shadows. Forgo the walks along the hedgerows and tangled
edges of Great Neck Point. Shun the woods and the rush-
guarded margins of the creek. Otherwise, as surely as blue jays will
steal eggs and hornworms infest the tomatoes, deerflies will also
make an instinctive response to spring's stern requirements.

The ravenous hordes descend without a sound. They circle
their quarry, then land, piercing flesh the instant they alight. Nor do
they cease to strike until their hunger has been satisfied. And, like
the legendary Amazons, every last one of this raging multitude is
female. The reclusive males loll idly elsewhere, feasting on pollen
and plant juices, committing careless acts of pollination while they
wait to fertilize the eggs of their own kind—eggs that can develop
only after the females are sated with blood. But after four weeks, no
later than the middle of June, the future of the species will have
been assured. Except for the occasional marauder, the deerflies disappear—until next year.

Coastal Carolinians aren't the only ones who are plagued by
these winged tormentors. A friend, an ardent angler who fishes out
West when he can, writes, "The only despicable creature I know is
the deerfly, which punctures my right hand, just as I'm trying to cast
a fly; I dearly love to squash them slowly." In his opinion, though
other forms of life, like snakes, qualify as thoroughly unlikable,
"Deerflies are really bad-ass." No region of North America offers
escape from deerflies; everywhere, from the East Coast to the West,
from the Rio Grande north into the Canadian Rockies, their various
species—all of them in the genus *Chrysops*, the "golden-eyes"—home
in on unprotected flesh and drink their blood meals. Their common
name refers to their preferred source of food: white-tailed and mule
deer. But lacking deer or other ungulates, they are perfectly satisfied
to feast on human victims. The head and neck are their favorite
zones of attack, and some, landing on the hair, will even try to burrow down to the scalp.

With all other true flies, from common houseflies and robber flies, bot- and blowflies to the daintier dance flies and flower-loving flies, the golden-eyes are members of the order Diptera, insects with "two wings." Most other insects boast two pairs of wings (though some, like silverfish and book lice, have none at all). In the Diptera, the second pair was anciently modified into a set of small organs, called halteres and shaped like narrow clubs, that are used as flight stabilizers. But where many kinds of flies vibrate their wings, zooming from here to there with a drone or a buzz, the golden-eyes opt for stealth and glide in on their prey with the silence of a moth. Their suborder is Brachycera—the "shorthorns"—a term that refers to their relatively short antennae. And the family is that of the Tabanidae, which they share with the physically larger, equally bloodthirsty horseflies; the family's name springs from *tabanus*, the Romans' generic word for any horsefly. That fly, a worldwide scourge, is represented by more than one hundred species in North America alone. *Tabanus americanus, T. punctifer, T. atratus, T. trimaculatus*—American horsefly, sting-bearing horsefly, black horsefly, three-spotted horsefly—the scientific name for each species usually refers to the insect's appearance or point of origin. One particularly vicious sort is commonly called a greeneye or greenie. Unlike its smaller deerfly cousins, which prefer a victim's upper reaches, it homes in on ankles and legs.

Oistros—that's the general word that the Greeks used for flies of this kind. And, in a time before time, it was just such a fly that inflicted divine retribution on the maiden Io, who had, without intent, attracted the lordly fancy of Zeus. But his wife, the lady Hera, took exception to putting up with yet another bout of philandering, and summoning the easy magic at her command, she turned Io into a cow. More than that, she sent an *oistros* winging after the now transformed object of her husband's lust. And *oistros*, often translated as gadfly, was nothing other than an aboriginal horsefly, perhaps the first one ever in the world. According to Aeschylus in his play *Suppliants*, this is what Hera and her *oistros* accomplished: when the fly found the cow (grazing placidly, no doubt, in some green meadow), it bit her, drawing blood, and bit her again, again, again until her hide was running red. Io, flystung and stampeded, ran for her life. She hurled herself the length of Asia, through cities and towns, through pastures and deserts. And in her mad flight, her body plundered by the winged drover's sharp bites, she transformed the landscape: valleys sank in her tracks, and mountains rose, rivers welled forth. At last she came to an Egyptian oasis sacred to Zeus. The people there were horror-struck at her appearance: a flyblown, half-human piece of patchflesh, here woman, there cow. Zeus saw her, of course, and took pity, restoring her to fully human form after he'd duly performed an act of insemination.

But the gods have left the world now and retreated into myth. It is Hera's *oistros* that has stayed behind, and its progeny, the tabanids—the legions of hairy horseflies, the myriad deerflies with dark or golden eyes—are with us today, still inflicting their bites, still feasting on our blood so that their kind shall endure.

How do they find us? The female tabanid, be she horsefly or deerfly, is not alerted by body heat, as ticks and chiggers are, but rather responds, like *oistros*, to the movement, the slink or stride or gallop, of the quarry. The harder Io ran, the faster and more furious was *oistros*'s pursuit. In the female tabanid's zeal for prey, she has been discovered to respond as well to other moving things, like cars and trains. And she's capable of speed; someone with a passion to know such things has clocked her flight at regularly more than twenty-five miles an hour. When prey appears, she homes in soundlessly. Nor is it only warm-blooded mammals that are chosen for a meal; some species of horseflies feed on reptiles, including alligators.

When contact is made, blood is instantly tapped through an incision made by the fly's mouthparts, which resemble a tiny wedge with scalpel-sharp edges. Blood welling freely, the fly soaks it up with the labellum, a spongelike segment of the lower lip. After such a meal, the deeply pierced victim often continues to bleed; livestock that are frequently attacked may forfeit their lives to the loss of blood. Meanwhile, the fly has hastened forth on silent wings to find a mate among the nectar-sipping males. (The enormous compound eyes of male tabanids touch along the midline, giving them the one-eyed aspect of a Cyclops.) After her eggs are fertilized, the female fly lays them on aquatic or streamside plants with leaves that overhang the water. And when the larvae hatch, they dine voraciously. Deerfly maggots eat only vegetables, like decaying wood, leaf mold, and beached pondweed, while their horsefly kin feed solely on meat, devouring such creatures as snails, worms, insects, and even frogs. Then, appetites satisfied for the nonce, they burrow in the mud and pupate; all of them overwinter, and some species go down for a long sleep that lasts two years. In spring, the adults emerge. The horseflies are large, robust, and furry, with eyes that often show an iridescent blue or green; the deerflies are smaller, their soft bodies striped tan and charcoal gray, their wings bearing dark calligraphic patterns, with eyes plain brown in some species but in others shiny gold or green zigzagged with red. On emergence, the females' stealthy and relentless quest for blood begins again.

Other biting flies exist: the midges, especially the no-see-ums, and the blackflies, scourge of Maine, that are bold and ravenous enough to sneak into a victim's sleeping bag. I feel almost fortunate that in Carolina I must contend every year only with several kinds of deerfly. One is *Chrysops vittatus*, the "banded golden-eye"; these are the fearless raiders with dark eyes and dark-patterned wings that haunt the woods and hedgerows. The other is a piratical species, no bigger than a housefly but with gleaming golden eyes, that works over the water near shore and strikes me as I fish the gill net. But I must swear and swat only for those blessedly brief four weeks in spring. The problem could be worse: in some circumstances, deerflies are vectors for eye diseases or tularemia, a plaguelike bacterial disease that afflicts wild animals, especially rabbits and rodents, but is transmitted from these hosts to human beings by fly bites.

And the problem could be even more dire. Some flies are

unapologetically more bad-ass than deer- and horseflies were ever designed to be. Compared to these prodigies, the tabanids are mere amateurs at the painful exploitation of prey. Consider the blowflies, the Calliphoridae, or "beautiful robbers," a name that encompasses both their parasitic behavior and also the gleaming metallic colors on the bodies of the family's typical members, the bluebottle and greenbottle flies. The larvae of most calliphorid species dine on dead tissue, but some, like the screwworm—*Cochliomyia hominivorax*, the "spirally twisted man-eating fly"—devour living flesh. Screwworm flies, once ubiquitous pests of cattle in the United States, were thought to have been eliminated through the release of laboratory-sterilized males and the subsequent reproductive failures in badly infested areas, but recently, in 1997, they were back at work in Texas, stowaways that came silently, deviously over the Mexican border under the hide of a dog.

(It's hard to admit that flies can be of service to us. So, I'll do it in a parenthetical whisper. The maggots of some calliphorid species have been used since time immemorial to cleanse wounds, a task they accomplish by eating dead, germ-laden tissue. Unknown to themselves, they also encourage healing by excreting a substance called allantoin, which is used as an active ingredient both in expensive over-the-counter cosmetics and in the kind of medicinal cream that patients undergoing radiation treatments for cancer may apply to affected skin to allay the effects of literally being cooked by high-intensity X-rays. The secret: allantoin not only fights bacteria but works to stimulate cell growth.)

In the bad-ass department, consider also the large tribe of botflies, one of which specializes in humankind. That one is *Dermatobia hominis*, "skin-creature of man," which is not equipped to deposit its eggs beneath the human hide and so enlists the help of other insects, like mosquitoes and biting flies. It lays its eggs on these carriers; when they bite, the warmth of the prey causes the eggs to hatch, and the newborn maggots then insinuate themselves into the bleeding wound. This tribe includes a gaggle of families, including the Gasterophilidae, the "stomach-loving" horse botflies; the Cuterebridae, the "skin-boring" robust botflies; and the Oestridae, the family of bot- and warble flies that is named (with scientific inexactness but a proper focus on the torment caused) for Hera's *oistros*. "Warble" has nothing to do with sound but rather refers to the subcutaneous swellings made in the flesh of cattle as the larvae of the ox warble fly grow and feast on the products—the pus and decayed flesh—of the irritation that they cause. The larvae of another oestrid develop in the nostrils of sheep. As for the gasterophilids, they lay their eggs on equine lips or nostrils, and when the horse licks them into its mouth, they travel to the stomach or intestines, where they hatch into maggots with a hunger great enough to debilitate the animal. In all these families, the larvae leave their nurseries within the host and drop to the ground to pupate.

Information about *Cuterebra*, the genus for which the cuterebrids were named, comes from my daughter Elisabeth, a veterinarian, who has seen the ravages its larvae cause in cats and dogs. (She also supplied the facts about the screwworm's dog-assisted reentry.) Nominally a parasite of rabbits and rodents, the skin-borer fly may sometimes jump those bounds in seeking to perpetuate its kind, sometimes affecting people as well as wild animals and pets. And the flies are large, often growing to twenty millimeters in length, while the maggots are downright huge, measuring in at twenty-five millimeters—more than an inch! A monster like that leaves behind a deep pit in its host's flesh when it drops out to pupate. My daughter names the species as the most despicable she knows.

"Supposing," I say to her, "there were no such thing as *Cuterebra*?"

"I'd see fewer cats and rabbits with holes in them, that's all," she replies.

I tell her that I can't imagine how they fit into the earth's puzzle pieces or what their purpose is, beyond ensuring a future from now to eternity for the skin borers. And I say, "*Cuterebra*—looks like the world could do without them."

"The world *could* do without them," she says. "But they're parasites. They cannot do without the world."

The same holds true for all the predatory and parasitic flies— the screws and bots, the deerflies and horseflies, the thousand detestable others. This May, on the first day that the bad-ass hordes come swarming in on silent wings, I'll mark my journal with a marginal sketch of a fly with dark patterns on its wings. I'll start counting down on the Four-Week War, and for twenty-eight days I shall swat and squash them with a pleasure equal, at least, to that of my fishing friend. And I shall remember that I don't need them, but in their lust for what I and my kind can supply, they do need us.

A FOOT IN THE DOOR

Destroying Angel (*Amanita virosa*)

The Fungi

WITHOUT any warning, without the slightest sound or motion, my childhood repossesses me. The ambush begins in the entrance hall of Rowan Oak, William Faulkner's 1840s plantation house in Oxford, Mississippi; it overwhelms me, whisks me away as I stand in the doorway of the writer's study scanning the outline, penciled on the walls in red and black, of his last book, *A Fable*. But I'm not really there. Instead, in a most physical way, I've been transported to the Shenandoah Valley in the era of World War II; I've been returned to my grandmother's high-ceilinged brick house, where I spent the war years while my father served overseas with the Army. There, summer and winter, the air smelled, as it does at Rowan Oak, of furniture polish, brass polish, and mold—most of all, mold.

That pervasive, primeval mustiness emanated from my grandmother's books—books in the breakfront, books on the mantel and in the walnut secretary, books in the Wernicke case that had long ago lost the glass doors protecting its shelves. *The Princess and the Goblin; The Water-Babies;* Bulfinch's *The Age of Fable* and collections of myths edited by Gayley and Guerber; a leather-bound Latin lexicon used by my great-uncle at Washington and Lee in 1888; and first editions, once my mother's, of *The Wonderful Wizard of Oz* and *The Road to Oz*—these are among the titles I remember or, in the case of the myths and lexicon, have appropriated and shelved among my own books to this day. Those volumes still bear the immemorial staleness on their foxed pages.

That smell haunts Faulkner's grand house. Barred by velvet ropes from entering the rooms, I cannot read the titles of his books, but I can see their full buckram or leather bindings, and the gilt lettering on their spines. Though it stands to reason that few, if any, are the same as those in my grandmother's smaller collection, the Mississippi books and hers are definitely kin. They are related not only by their production in Victorian times or the early 1900s but also by the fact that both libraries have been similarly affected by enduring summer after summer in the land of mockingbirds, gentility, and heat combined with high humidity. The cloth and paper of these volumes are filled with fusty memories of dripping, sweltering summers, and, without the drying effects of air-conditioning, they receive a new infusion of moisture every year. Of course, more moisture promotes more mold.

There's a technical term for the action of mold on books, the foxing and splotching, the greenish patches that sprout on the covers, and the eternally dank smell: tropical deterioration. One does not have to be in the tropics, however, to note these phenomena; all that's needed is a cozy steam bath of warmth and humidity—behold! Last summer, on the sticky, hot Carolina coast, the wide, nylon-webbing collar of a dog four years dead came to light as I was cleaning out a dresser drawer (why, against all the urgings of good sense, do we keep these reminders of heartbreak?); the collar, originally brown, was coated thickly with turquoise mold. And not only nylon and paper are attacked but also fabric of all kinds, leather, lumber and living woods, bark, leaves, seeds, and insects both dead and alive. So are shower curtains, rubber duckies and spandex shorts, electrical insulation, kerosene-based aviation fuel, and just about everything else in the whole wide world. Nothing of organic origin is immune.

But molds are hardly confined to the warmer places on the earth. Some are drought resistant and enter a dormant state until the rains finally come. Others live only in the water as parasites on aquatic life. Like goblins or the tiger that hides under the bed, most work at highest efficiency in the dark. And a varied group known as psychrophiles—cold-lovers—is even known to thrive in the winter-long darkness of both the Arctic and the Antarctic. As for their local success in surviving near-freezing conditions, anyone with a refrigerator knows what happens to the leftovers that have migrated back into the nether regions. Mashed potatoes turn pink; cream cheese grows gray-green fur; brown specks blossom abundantly in the applesauce. Wherever molds appear, they take over, nor can they be easily dislodged.

The reason for these silent and ubiquitous encroachments is, of course, perpetuation of the species—as many as 250,000 of them according to several estimates. The molds are inescapable; everywhere across the planet they help themselves to an over-spilling cornucopia of opportunities that satisfy their appetites and enable them to reproduce. And together they constitute a biological kingdom, the Fungi, until recently thought to be an odd and populous offshoot of the plant kingdom but now recognized as a distinct realm of its own. Fungus and mold—the words applied to the realm's inhabitants are well-nigh interchangeable, though the former comes from a Latin transformation of a Greek word for sponge and the latter first fell bluntly from an Anglo-Saxon tongue.

Mold or fungus (use the term you prefer), the kingdom's popu-lace falls into five sometimes overlapping classes. It was thought until recently that a sixth group, the slime molds, was part of the realm, but it has been reassigned to the kingdom of the Protista, which it shares with organisms like the diatoms and dinoflagel-lates. The remaining five all have polysyllabic Greek names: Phycomycetes, or weed fungi, which includes the two divisions Mastigomycotina and Zygomycotina; Ascomycetes; Basid-iomycetes, and Fungi Imperfecti, also known as Deuteromycotina. The suffixes -*mycetes* and -*mycotina* simply mean "fungi," and the rest of these tongue twisters denominate the five respectively as whip and yoke (the two divisions of the weeds), skin, pedestal, and imperfect or secondary fungi. Each tribe performs a multiplicity of jobs. One species of whip, for example, attacks fish in aquaria—the dreaded "ich"; another causes potato blight. The whip that infests potatoes is *Phytophthora infestans*—"plant corrupter," and it alone was responsible for the wholesale putrefaction in the fields that led to Ireland's five gaunt years of famine, beginning in 1845. The yokes may be blamed for pin molds on food and leather. The skins, so called for the sacs in which they encase their spores, include baker's and brewer's yeast, the splendidly edible morels, and the cup fungi that grow on wood. The pedestals tend to have a base supporting a cap; these are the typical toadstools and mushrooms, though the group also encompasses bracket fungi and the no-neck puffballs that balloon straight out of the ground. Some pedestals form fairy rings, some glow with cold luminescence, some are hallucinogenic, still others produce toxins that kill. The imperfects lack the capability for sexual reproduction (note the taxonomical value judgment here); several species of imperfects are used as agents for ripening cheeses, like the blue-veined Roquefort and the green Gorgonzola, while others play humanly counterproductive roles, causing ringworm and athlete's foot. And within each tribe dwell species that are strictly parasitic, bound to feed on the tissues of a live host; strictly sapro-phytic, obliged to eat dead matter; or opportunistic, switching from one mode to the other in order to take advantage of the nutrients available, be they alive or dead.

All of the fungi, no matter their tribe, seem to plague rather than please us. Some animals, to be sure, draw benefit from their existence; several species of ants and beetles assure themselves of a steady food supply by farming fungi, and the endangered red-cock-aded woodpeckers could hardly drill their cavity-nests in old-growth pines if not for the molds that soften old heartwood with rot. As for humankind, we do honor the outright edibility—raw, sautéed, or stuffed—of a few fungi, and appreciate their invaluable assistance in the preparation of foods like bread, cheeses, and the famous sauces Worcestershire and soy. The molds are friends not only of the gourmet but of the tippler, too, for it is they that stimu-late the fermentation that results in hard cider, stout, and lager, wines both sweet and dry, Bombay Sapphire, Jack Daniels, and all other forms of potable alcohol. (As for other forms of service to mankind, a parenthetical acknowledgment should probably be made of *Empusa musca*—"fly-digester"—a mold that's parasitic on the com-mon housefly.) And when it comes to sickness or health, where would we be without drugs like penicillin, ergotine, and strepto-mycin? By their name, you can tell that all of the -mycin antibiotics are derived from fungus, for *mykos* is the Greek word for mushroom, with the hard *k* softened to *c* in the suffix.

But there's nothing soft in human perceptions of the Fungi and their work. We know their devastations well: Dutch elm disease; American chestnut blight; mycotoxins killing cattle and poultry; myriad fungal infections decimating crops; ergotism, or St. Anthony's fire, leading to loss of human limbs; histoplasmosis affecting human lungs; and a hideous host of other damaging or fatal ills, including mycotismus, which is the fancy clinical term for mushroom poisoning. The everyday words that have been used in English for a thousand years demonstrate an ineradicable human suspicion of the Fungi, and an aboriginal dislike, not to mention terror at the threats they pose to crops and, so, to human life. Listen to the no-nonsense curtness, the thud and hiss of these terms: blight, blotch, bunt, mold, mildew, rot, rust, scurf, smut, and wilt. With the exception of the very last, all are ancient Teutonic words that hit the ear like imprecations. Wilt, the odd word out, first rose on American tongues in the mid-1800s. It certainly provides a graphic description of what happens to tomato vines set in mold-infested soil. Mold enters through their roots and rises, clogging their water-conducting vascular systems; vines shooting sturdily upward one day are drooping and wizened the next, and dead the week after. Northern Europeans and Americans, however, are hardly alone in their appraisal of the harm that Fungi do. The Romans nominated a god of rust, Robigus, and, lest grain be blighted before it could be reaped, attempted to appease him with an annual festival, the Robigalia, held on April 25. And, should a Roman suffer poisoning from eating fungus, the natural historian Pliny (A.D. 23–79) offered a long list of antidotes, from radishes and twice-boiled cabbage to lily roots and the lees of wine. But no remedy, natural or otherwise, kept the emperor Claudius from succumbing in A.D. 54 to mycotismus. Unwittingly, he ate toxic fungi especially selected for him by his wife Agrippina. Of that occasion, Pliny remarked that, as things turned out, a worse poison had been left behind: Claudius's son and successor Nero.

Mushrooms—in his 1597 *Herball*, the English botanist John Gerard called them "bastard plants" and "earthie excrescences" and pronounced that "some are very venemous and full of poison, others not so noisome; and neither of them very wholesome meate." Gerard's contemporary Shakespeare went even farther in *King Lear* by assigning a prime cause to the Fungi, and especially to the rusts, bunts, and stinking smuts that swell and rot cereal crops and can also poison people who eat infected grains. Edgar, the rightful but dispossessed heir of the Earl of Gloucester, acts the madman, staggering from a hut and howling his credentials as a lunatic: "This is the foul fiend Flibbertigibbet: he begins at curfew, and walks till the first cock; he gives the web and the pin, squints the eye, and makes the harelip, mildews the white wheat, and hurts the poor creature of earth." So, it's Flibbertigibbet's fault that mold, doing little good but much harm, has silently helped itself to worldwide dominion and engages in its stealthy enterprises not just between curfew and cock-crow but from sunup to sundown as well.

There's no stopping the foul fiend, no escaping his excrescences, the Fungi. For, they are surely the planet's most successful reproductive strategists. Asexually, a single cell may attenuate itself, branching and budding to produce a mycelium—the threadlike food-obtaining structure—that reaches out for feet, yards, acres; each portion is genetically identical to every other. We've all seen the tatters, the frayed gauze of various mycelia clinging to damp ground, rotting wood, and those back-of-beyond refrigerator experiments. This kind of cell may also divide and send out spores, each of which contains the potential for a faithful clone of its parent. Then, the organism may leave behind the celibate life and become a fully sexual entity. The rusts, of which there may be four to five thousand species (not many as molds go), are characterized by a modus vivendi called pleomorphism—the adoption of multiple forms. They are also characterized by dependence on alternate hosts—gooseberry or currant and pines, for example, or barberry and wheat. In its sexual phase, on the currant or barberry where it overwinters, a rust contains gametes. These are sex cells properly called pycniospores, or "close-packed spores," each with a single haploid nucleus—that are analogous to the egg and sperm of animals. (Why only analogous, not the same, is an amazing matter that I'll come to shortly.) After sexual fusion takes place, aeciospores—"assaulting spores"—are formed, with each containing two nuclei, one from each pycniospore; these aeciospores establish a mycelium. From that network, crop after crop of urediospores—"blighting spores"—arises and becomes a windborne plague, leaving the first host to infect the second. After the damage is done, teliospores—"final spores" (that aren't truly final)—are produced; some may germinate forthwith, some sleep through the winter, but in all of them the two nuclei fuse. The germination of teliospores leads to the last phase of the cycle, the sporidia—"small spores"—which are also called basidiospores, a word that means "pedestal spores." Wind bears the sporidia back to the alternate host—from wheat to barberry, pine to currant—where they grow into mycelia, from which arise the picnia that produce the sexually active pycniospores.

Sex among the Fungi, what a peculiar phenomenon! Or so it may seem to us who are accustomed to think of mating in terms of male and female, each with its own gender-specific set of genes. But in the voiceless, covert kingdom of the molds, a multiplicity of genders, or mating types, holds sway. It is known that each has not one but two sets of genes, though how they work is still a mystery. And each mating type may contain a humanly bewildering array of variants. Sexual fusion is impossible only between types possessing an identical array. The possibilities for fusion, though, are boggling. If one type has twenty variants, and the other two hundred, then twenty times two hundred combinations can occur, for an orgiastic total of four thousand. Why such complexity? One notable mycologist has pointed out that for species divided into male and female, only half the population is available to each gender for the establishment of a fertile union, but with multiple variants the molds have maximized their chances for meeting a suitable partner in the subterranean dark. Nor do fungal peculiarities stop with this huge enhancement of the odds in the mating game. When male and female animals pair, sperm unites with egg, and the single sets of chromosomes in each—the haploid sets—fuse into a diploid set, from which the embryo develops. But when molds mate, fusion is delayed, and the nuclei remain separated until the moment that a fully mature specimen puts forth its spores. The reason for delay may have to do with retaining the possibility for multiple partners, for fusion with other wandering mycelial threads, and thus for assuring the various perfect species of genetic diversity on a truly grand scale.

Success is the Fungi's reason for being. The envoys of Flibbertigibbet care nothing about ripening cheeses or blighting elms, feeding ants or causing the tender skin between our toes to itch and peel. Instead, as Sylvia Plath puts it in her poem "Mushrooms," *"Our kind multiplies:/We shall by morning/Inherit the earth./Our foot's in the door."* Multiply they have, and not just the pedestal mushrooms about which she writes, but every last member of the realm. More than that, their mycelia, if not their feet, have reached far beyond the door; they've gained the equator, they're found at the poles, they've entered almost every cranny in between. And it is not unimaginable that if an asteroid sends our kind the way of the dinosaurs, or if we're suicidal enough to envelop ourselves in the mushroom clouds of nuclear warfare, the Fungi will survive whatever cataclysm wipes us out.

Meanwhile, they scavenge as they've always done. They, more than the selective vultures, more than the picky hyenas and hagfish, are angels of decay. They not only consume the things we treasure, like books, tomato vines, and old dog collars, but are able to ingest every bit of the world's organic trash. In the vastness of their hunger lies usefulness and also something to admire.

And something else arose from the moldy books at Rowan Oak, and the musty fabrics: they took me to another time, another place, another recognition—part grudging, part not—that there are lives above, below, and quite beyond those of my kind.

Fly Amanita (*Amanita muscaria*)

THE CREATURE
WITH NINETEEN
LIVES

Opossum (*Didelphis marsupialis*)

Common Opossum

ONCE upon a time, in another life three decades ago, I lived with husband and school-aged children in a big house on a large lot with woods and New England stone walls. And my husband, who was not in any way an animal lover, promised the children that they might keep as pets whatever wildlife they happened to catch on our grounds. Out, then, with the collecting jars, nets, and a Havahart trap. The results: uncountable fireflies, monarch caterpillars, a bullfrog or two, a ring-necked snake, a half-grown cat, and an opossum. The cat and frogs were let go, the snake (a fragile species) died, the caterpillars were fed until they pupated and later burst forth as butterflies, and the 'possum made the father of my children rescind his promise. They put it in a fifty-gallon aquarium, though, and kept it for a week, feeding it table scraps and listening to its hisses of complaint.

I remember the catching and caging of the 'possum. It had a long bare tail, coarse gray body fur, hairless black ears, and a white face that culminated in an eraser-pink nose. I remember its teeth, too—long, pointy things covered with a green scum that may have been algae. I also remember thinking and saying that it wasn't really the kind of animal that made a decent house pet. Hey, children, let that critter go. They did after that long week, and I thought about 'possums rarely after that. Only recently, when someone named the opossum as her top candidate for the most despicable species on earth and clinched the nomination with a wide-eyed shiver, did the image of this animal resurface. Now it won't go away. The only way to exorcise its presence in my mind is to investigate it and uncover its secrets.

What could be despicable about the common opossum? Those green teeth, all fifty of them. The coarse, tatty-looking grayish fur. The long, tough, quite naked terminal appendage, which is monstrously rodentlike. Then, given the chance (a loose-fitting lid), it plunders garbage cans as eagerly as any 'coon. And my neighbor Mo Wixon, aged seventy-seven and wise in the ways of critters and plants, once went to war against 'possumkind. He was raising red worms, mighty popular with fishermen, in a bunch of old refrigerators turned on their backs. He says, still irritated by the memory,

"Those 'possums would get in there and just gobble up my worms. I had to knock a couple of 'em in the head."

Looks and habits apart, the animal is often seen either as a creature of Walt Kelly—Pogo the 'possum, eternally adorable and wise—or as a primitive life-form notable for its stupidity and thus the butt of jokes like this one: Why did the chicken cross the road? To show the 'possum it could be done. 'Possum lives in light verse, too. My grandmother's scrapbook contains this ditty, "In the Georgia Woods," which was published by the *Atlanta Constitution* a decade or so after the beginning of the twentieth century:

> The snarlin' o' the 'possum,
>> The boundin' o' the buck,
> Barkin' o' the squirrel,
>> An' the rabbit's foot for luck,
>
> Like a fiddle's music
>> When it knows the tune to play,
> But a rifle's ringin' echo
>> Beats a fiddle any day.
>
> An' the whirrin' o' the partridge—
>> Then there's music in the air,
> An' 'possum served for supper
>> Beats a hotel bill o' fare.

Then, along with raccoon, jay, and other rural creatures, 'possum also inhabits at least one folk song, "Bile Them Cabbage Down." In one rollicking verse, raccoon, on the ground below a persimmon tree, directs 'possum, who is already up there, to "shake them 'simmons down." With that, it's fair to say that the opossum does not suffer from a picky appetite but relishes fruit along with other delectables like fishing worms, insects, birds' eggs, birds themselves, mice, and the kitchen scraps found in garbage cans. And it sometimes behaves like a four-footed vulture, eating carrion as it can, but more about this predilection shortly.

'Possum also inhabits the historical record. In 1612, Captain

John Smith, describing the wildlife of the Virginia colony, had this to say: "An Opassum hath a head like a swine and a taile like a Rat and is of the bignes of a Cat. Under her belly she hath a bagge, wherein she lodgeth, carrieth, and sucketh her young." Nothing remotely similar had ever been seen in Europe; so he borrowed the animal's Algonquian Indian name, wrote it down as best he could, and gave it to the world.

And so began the wondering European references to "'possum." Nearly a century after Captain Smith's day, John Lawson, gentleman surveyor, traveled the Carolinas and wrote of all that he saw, from eagles and polecats to oaks and 'simmon trees and on to the Indians, their manners and customs. The resulting book, A New Voyage to Carolina, was published in 1709 as an inducement to potential colonists to cross the ocean and settle in ever fair, ever fertile "Summer-Country." And Lawson was always keen at noting the peculiarities of the things that he came across: a hollow tulip poplar that once gave a man and his furniture ample living space; the Indian habit of feeding a child roasted "Rearmouse"—a bat, that is—as a cure for pica; the "excrementious Matter" that forms the rattles of a rattlesnake's tail; and the edibility, yea or nay, of every bird he came across. He commented also on the edibility of 'possum, which he sampled happily in South Carolina when his party ran short of victuals: "The Weather was very cold, the Winds holding *Northerly*. We made ourselves as merry as we could, having a good Supper with the Scraps of Venison we had given us by the *Indians*, having kill'd 3 Teal and a Possum; which Medly all together made a curious Ragoo." His detailed description of 'possum shows clearly that he found the living animal to be a whole sight more curious than this gamey stew:

> The *Possum* is found no where but in *America*. He is the Wonder of all the Land-Animals, being the size of a Badger and near that Colour. The Male's Pizzle is placed retrograde; and in time of Coition, they differ from all other Animals, turning Tail to Tail, as Dog and Bitch when ty'd. The Female, doubtless, breeds her Young at her Teats; for I have seen them stick fast thereto, when

they have been no bigger than a small Raspberry, and seemingly inanimate. She has a Paunch, or false Belly, wherein she carries her Young, after they are from those Teats, till they can shift for themselves. Their food is Roots, Poultry, or wild Fruits. They have no hair on their Tails, but a sort of a Scale, or hard Crust, as the Bevers have. If a Cat has nine lives, this Creature surely has nineteen; for if you break every Bone in their Skin, and mash their Skull, leaving them for Dead, you may come an hour after, and they will be gone quite away, or perhaps you meet them creeping away. They are a very stupid Creature, utterly neglecting their Safety. They are the most like Rats of any thing. I have, for Necessity in the Wilderness, eaten of them. Their Flesh is very white, and well-tasted; but their ugly Tails put me out of Conceit with that Fare. They climb Trees as the Raccoons do. Their Fur is not esteem'd nor used, save that the *Indians* spin it into Girdles and Garters.

My friend Mo tells me that he's also out of conceit with that fare and would prefer hotel food any time. "I've seen people singeing off the hair in a bonfire before cooking the beast," he says. "But when I was a child on the farm, lightning would strike a horse or cow, and it'd just lie there. And every time you'd walk by the old dead cow, there'd go a 'possum out the debris chute, or the fantail, so to speak. It was hard to eat them after that."

As it happens, John Lawson has fed us a Ragoo of fact and supposition, along with mention of some typically eighteenth-century bone-breaking and skull-mashing (no animal-rights groups in those days). Lawson was off the mark on the location of teats and "paunch" but right about the retrograde pizzle and the ugly tail. He was dead wrong, as shall be seen, about the animal's stupidity. But his statement that 'possum is the "Wonder of all the Land-Animals" is hardly an exaggeration.

For the common opossum, sometimes called the Virginia opossum, is indeed a wonder. Formally, the animal is known as *Didelphis marsupialis*, the "marsupial double womb." That double womb is an anatomical phenomenon in the same odd league as the retrograde pizzle. But first, a look at the place of 'possum in the scheme of things. 'Possum belongs to a most peculiar order of mammals, the Marsupialia, which might be translated as "pouch beasts" for the pocketlike flap of skin—*marsupium* in Latin—that covers the nipples of females in many, though not all, species. Marsupials first appeared in the Cretaceous period; the oldest fossils come from North America and date back some eighty million years. Fossils of an animal almost identical to the present-day *D. marsupialis* go back a not inconsiderable sixty-five million years. As marsupials evolved, some of them were vulpine and some hyenalike, with bone-crushing teeth, while others grew as large as a modern-day rhinoceros. The carnivorous, jaguar-sized *Thylascosmilus* that once prowled what is now South America, sported long, powerful canine teeth, which it used for killing prey. In fact, it filled the niche occupied elsewhere by the sabertoothed cat and became extinct when the land bridge between North and South America was reestablished about ten million years ago and the sabertooth, a more canny predator, moved south into the stomping grounds of *Thylacosmilus*. Marsupials have since made themselves at home in two parts of the planet. Some 170 present-day species are native to Celebes, Timor, New Guinea, and, most notably, Australia, famed for its koalas, wallabies, kangaroos, bandicoots, Tasmanian devils, and a varied bunch of forest-dwelling creatures called possums. Those possums, noted by eighteenth-century European explorers like Captain James Cook, came to share the name of the earlier discovered North American 'possum because of their general kinship as marsupials; they are otherwise not closely related. Australian possums belong to the Phalangeridae, the pha-langer family, so named for its phalanges—its toes—which have evolved so that the first and second digits on the hind feet are opposable and can be used to grasp branches as the animals travel through their arboreal habitat (the North American opossum can do this, too). Some phalanger species have developed flaps of skin between their fore and hind limbs, which can be spread to help them sail through the air in the manner of a flying squirrel.

The New World houses only two marsupial families, totalling seventy species, more or less. They include such creatures as the rat opossum, or selva, which has no pouch; the four-eyed opossum, which wears two large white spots over its eyes; and the yapok, or water opossum, which leads a semiaquatic life and so has been blessed with webbed toes, oily fur, and a pouch that can be tightly closed to keep its offspring dry. All these live in Central or South America. The only one of the seventy that has ventured north is *D. marsupialis*, the common opossum. Though it ranges as far below the equator as Argentina, it has made itself thoroughly at home in not only the United States but southern Canada as well.

But no matter the land it travels through, *D. marsupialis* (called 'possum from here on) is indeed a most surpassing wonder. It raises a sense of wonder, too, in anyone who contemplates the inventive ways in which the marsupials—also called metatherians, or "early beasts"—diverge from the placental mammals, which are sometimes dubbed eutherians, or "good beasts." (There seems to be some taxonomical snobbishness at work here.) The main features that bring marsupials into the mammal camp are, of course, warm-bloodedness, at least some body hair, and mammary glands that produce milk for suckling the live-born young. (There's an exception, however, to prove the rule: the kind of mammals known as prototherians, or "first beasts." These are the duck-billed platypuses and the echidnas, or spiny anteaters, sole members of the order Monotremata—the "single holes," for their combined intestinal-urinary-genital tract, or cloaca. They lay eggs but suckle their young after hatching. Because the females have no nipples, the young absorb milk through the skin.) Another characteristic that 'possum shares with many eutherian mammals is that it gets about on four legs. Most important, like every other living creature, mammal or not—no matter whether they fly or swim, wriggle or leap, skitter or walk—'possum lives to perpetuate its kind, to keep a basic 'possumhood alive on earth. But from there it goes its own peculiar way.

Take that naked, crusty-looking tail, which stretches out for half the creature's total length. It's prehensile. Despite common wisdom, it's used hardly at all as a hook for hanging upside down but serves rather as an anchor to steady the animal as it moves about on the branches of trees. The tail is also handy for toting materials for building the nests in which this mainly nocturnal animal sleeps during the daytime; 'possum scoops up grass and leaves with mouth and front feet, then pushes them rearward to the tail, which curls around them like a carrying strap. Add to the prehensile tail the clawless, opposable digits on each of the hind feet: 'possum ranges through its arboreal habitat with the greatest of safety and ease. It nonetheless seems to prefer ambling about on the ground and is more often found on terra firma than aloft. Should 'possum encounter a copperhead or rattler in its perambulations, it falters not, nor does it flinch, for it is a creature endowed with an extraordinary resistance to snake venom. Then, contemplate 'possum's mouth, which can open more than ninety degrees, almost as great a gape as a rattlesnake's, and look, too, at the fifty teeth—far more of them than are granted other kinds of mammal. 'Possum's skull is specially constructed to handle the stresses created when so many teeth crunch down (John Lawson and friends must have discovered that it was far from easy to mash such a hard head). Its brain, however, is on the small side when compared to the brains of what are sometimes called the "higher mammals." Its body temperature ranges far lower than that of most mammals—94.5 degrees Fahrenheit, as compared to the human 98.6, the mouse's 100.2, and the 101.5 of cows and pigs. 'Possum has thus been relegated to the lower ranks of mammalkind. Such seeming underendowment may help account for pronouncements, like Lawson's, that 'possum is a "very stupid Creature." And its pizzle is indeed placed retrograde, just as Lawson said, with the scrotal sac located in front of the penis. What's more, the penis is forked.

Ah, but with good reason. The animal's most dramatic divergence from other kinds of mammals lies in its reproductive arrangements. Note, to begin with, the double womb that led to the naming of the whole New World family, the Didelphidae, to which the common opossum belongs. Each female has two uteruses, each served by its own vagina. The male's two-pronged penis is supported by a two-pronged cartilage, the didelphid equivalent of the penis bone found in every male mammal except for the primates. This arrangement makes very good sense because, with a fork in each vagina, the chances for fertilization are maximized.

One female common opossum may carry as many as two dozen embryos, not all of which make it to adulthood; an average litter numbers seven to nine. Gestation takes about thirteen days, with the walls of the yolk sacs of the developing young attached to the mother in a rudimentary fashion that is nonetheless placental, for it allows for the transfer of nourishment from mother to fetuses. But when the young are born, they arrive in the world not through the double vaginas but through a birth canal that develops for the occasion between the vaginas. The babies, for all that they are blind, naked, and tiny as grubs, come equipped with clawed fore-limbs that enable them to scrabble to the mother's pouch and latch for dear life on to her teats, which number thirteen. Not all succeed in reaching this destination; others may be out of luck because all available slots are already occupied. But those that do attain pouch-dom are kept in place by nipples that expand in the mouths of the newborns to form a firm bond. My friend Mo comes up with a bit of folk wisdom: "When they were raiding my worms and I knocked them over the head, there was one had four-five-six babies in her pouch. You know, they pull on the tit so hard it elongates. It was a good three inches." He's right about the length but wrong about the reason—it is maternal biology, not juvenile suction, that accounts for the three inches. (The expansion of the nipples also allows the newborn young of pouchless marsupials, like the selva, to hang on tight.) The babies will then stay in the mother's pouch for four or five weeks before they first crawl out. They are not completely independent then, for weaning does not take place till one hundred days after birth. But once out in the world, they sometimes cling to the fur on their mother's back and ride along as she meanders through her night's work. These little hitchhikers have also been known to return to the pouch for protection and milk.

And still no end to reproductive wonders. The female 'possum may remate within a few days of the birth of her young. But if these young have reached her pouch and are suckling, then the new fetuses will enter a state called embryonic diapause, a sort of suspended animation, in which fetal development stops until the pouch is once again empty and ready to receive the next generation. Usually, two litters are born each year.

'Possum may not seem bright. Beady-eyed and long-tailed, it lumbers along with apparent lethargy. There's also the notorious business of playing 'possum to which John Lawson refers: when confronted with danger, the animal goes belly up in an almost fatalistic fashion but creeps away as soon as danger disappears. It can maintain this deathlike quiescence for up to six hours. And there are those teeth, that bristling mouthful of green and pointy teeth. But Mo says, "An opossum is not near as vicious as people would think—hissing like a snake. You can just pick it up."

There is, however, one aspect of 'possum that may be considered truly despicable, especially by people who own horses or keep stables. 'Possum is the definitive host, the host sine qua non, of a protozoan, *Sarcocystis falcatula*, or "hook-shaped fleshy cyst." It is sometimes known as *S. neurona*, "found in the neurons," for the site it inhabited when it was first identified in horses. 'Possum ingests the protozoan when it eats intermediate hosts, like grackles and cowbirds; the microorganism takes hold and matures; 'possum then sends it into the world by way of feces. 'Possum is not affected in any way, but should a horse eat contaminated grain or graze in a pasture where 'possum has trod, it may become infested by the protozoan and suffer a disabling illness called equine protozoal myeloencephalitis, EPM for short, which causes brain lesions, convulsions, and sometimes death. 'Possum is not aware, of course, of its role as vector. All that hippophiles can do is try to eliminate the marsupial from the premises.

Given the intricacies of 'possumhood, it's unwise at best to call 'possum stupid. Consider its haunts. Think of its nineteen lives. It lives in story, song, and jingle-jangle verse, in joke and comic strip. It dwells in the notes of explorers and the digs of paleontologists. More significantly, it spends the rest of its lives in the tangible world, ever reconnoitering woods, fields, and yards, ever rambling in its own good time across the continent. It sequesters itself within the carcasses of livestock and wildlife. And were Mo still raising red worms, it would surely visit his refrigerators, there to fill its belly and stay fit for the overwhelmingly important business of bringing more 'possums into the world.

That's precisely what it has done with noteworthy success for, lo, sixty-five million years. John Lawson and others to the contrary, no animal that has kept its kind going for so long can possibly be considered stupid. To be sure, it has no knowledge of matters like time and longevity, nor does it care. But our own come-lately species, which knows and cares, might find another wonder here: any animal blessed with such an indomitable ability to survive, come glaciers or global warming, is a very clever animal indeed.

THE RIDDLES OF
THE SPHINX

Tomato Hornworm (*Manduca quinquemaculata*)

Hornworms

A mild June morning at Great Neck Point on North Carolina's wide and salty river Neuse—perfect for picking green beans. Five-gallon bucket in hand, I go to the vegetable garden and set to work. Three gallons along, when I stretch and look up, scanning the rows of beans and adjacent tomatoes, there it is, only an arm's length away—a hornworm. I can see its jaws move. It's chomping vigorously, implacably on the leaf of a Better Boy vine. In its wake lie the shorn stumps of other leaves.

Anyone who fancies homegrown, sun-ripened tomatoes (the only kind worth eating) is well acquainted with hornworms. Where tomatoes grow, there also flourish great, fleshy, spike-tailed eating machines. Nor do the vines attract only the kind known as the tomato hornworm but cater as well to the appetites of several closely related caterpillar species that also favor chowing down on the Solanaceae, the nightshade family, which includes potatoes and eggplant among its domesticated members. The caterpillar now devouring my plants—a pudgy thing as big around as my thumb—is a tobacco hornworm, *Manduca sexta*, the "six-spotted glutton," so named for its fierce appetite and the six orange spots on each side of the abdomen of its moth. The giveaway to its identification is the "horn," the stiff, backward-jutting spine on its nether end. That of the tomato hornworm, *Manduca quinquemaculata*, the "five-spotted glutton," is green with a black edge, but this one glows red as a burning ember. I know that the rest of its body is grossly corpulent and bright green, the better to hide amid the leafy fodder as it munches its way toward metamorphosis. And its sides are marked with seven white slashes, while those of the tomato hornworm are patterned with eight white patches, each shaped like a streamlined L. Today, however, I can see only the caterpillar's tail, not the markings on its body, for as it was eating away at my vines, something else was eating it: tiny spindles wound with white thread protrude from its skin and nearly cover it—the cocoons of braconid wasps. The green beans are patient; they will wait. I break the leaf from the vine and carry it inside, hornworm and all, to take a photograph.

Braconid: the name means, roughly, "short stuff" and refers to the minuscule size of the wasps in this family. The larvae of some braconids are parasitic on the larval stages of other kinds of insects. Braconids are found worldwide. Many species of the tiny wasps, most of them stingless and all belonging to the genus *Apanteles*, the "imperfect ones," are native to the New World, and they are fierce natural predators on the pests of New World plants like tobacco and tomatoes; other braconids have been introduced from Europe to help control the ravages of insects on cash crops like cabbages. The species at work on my hornworm turns out to be *A. congregatus*, the "assembled-congregated-swarming imperfect ones," so named for the numerous cocoons often seen on a single host. The adult wasps lay their eggs on the victim's skin. When the eggs hatch, the larvae burrow into their host, feasting until it's time to chew back up to the surface, on which they then spin their delicate cocoons. Devoured from the inside out, infested caterpillars invariably die, though they are ravenous, their great jaws working furiously, until the end. The wasps may not emerge from their pupae until well after the host's death. Nature is not only red in tooth and claw but also relentless in jaw and ovipositor.

When I return to the vegetable garden after taking *M. sexta's* picture, memory diverts me from the tedium of picking beans, thousands of beans. Once upon a time, at my children's behest, we kept tomato hornworms, the species with a green spine, under glass for observation. Oh, the see-through wonders of glass: guppies and angelfish in an aquarium, woodland plants—with occasional insects and frogs—in a terrarium, and tomato hornworms in the largest possible size of applesauce jar. The point of the exercise was, of course, to watch the caterpillar transform itself into a moth. (We kept smaller caterpillars, too—monarchs, black swallowtails, Polyphemus moths—but they were housed in appropriately smaller jars as we awaited chrysalis or cocoon and, later, wings.) For every hornworm, the big jar would be furnished with four or five inches of soil from the garden. In, then, with the caterpillar, and on with the lid, punched full of air holes. The lid would be removed, usually more than once daily, for the insertion of a fresh batch of tomato leaves to satisfy the hornworm's gargantuan appetite. And when the body showed rolls of flesh and the green skin seemed ready to burst, the chewing would stop, the great jaws become still at last. But the rest of the caterpillar would go into feverish action, loping around, around, around in its cage of glass. For days on end, it would explore perimeter and surface. Then, according to some internal cue, it would tunnel into the soil and there slough its skin. I learned later that there is a timetable for these events: four preliminary molts; then, when the creature's weight reaches seven grams, it starts its restless peregrinations and on the fourth day burrows and undergoes a fifth molt from worm to pupa. We could not always see the dark-brown pupa and its long tongue case, curving like the handle of a tall pitcher. We never saw the emergence of its moth (though we succeeded every time with monarch, swallowtail, and Polyphemus). Does hornworm require a long period of pupation? Did our hopes outrun our patience? Or did the kitchen counter simply need to be cleared of an in-the-way applesauce jar? At this remove, I do not know.

The experience of my husband, the Chief, with hornworms was of entirely another order. He never thought of keeping them as live zoological specimens, no indeed. He murdered them, and with malice aforethought. Nor was he unlike other sons of North Carolina farmers, who sent their children into the brightleaf tobacco fields as soon as they were five or six years old. Some summers he was sent off to his uncle's farm, which offered precisely the same kind of outdoor entertainment. There and at home, he and the other young'uns cropped the sandlugs—picked the dirt-covered bottom leaves, that is, the leaves too close to the ground for a grown man to gather easily. The young'uns cropped the higher leaves, too, and topped the plants, cutting off the blossom stems that jut high above the leaves. They'd come out of the fields covered with gummy tobacco sap that turned black as it dried. The Chief's aunt would then dole out what she called "weak, dirty tobacco hugs"—light, brief, arm's-length pats made only after a search for the least gummy place on the recipient. After this greeting, the kids would be made to take off their shirts and scrub down before they were allowed back in the house. But cropping and topping were only two aspects of the job. Another was pest removal. Like other tobacco fieldhands of tender years, the Chief was given a Mason jar partly filled with kerosene and dispatched to walk the rows inspecting them for hornworms; each one he found would be plucked off and plopped into the oily fluid. When the jar was crammed with fat green bodies, he'd dump them at field's edge and set off again with a refill of kerosene. Though kerosene alone would have done the trick, that wasn't the end. Because the youngest children weren't allowed to handle fire, an older hand, aged ten or so, would strike a match and send the kerosene-soaked hornworms off in a great, leaping, popping, pyromaniacal blaze of glory. But that was more than half a century ago. Nowadays, pesticides do the worms in.

As the adage puts it, beauty lies in the eye of the beholder. So does the opposite, and try as I may, my eye discovers no beauty in hornworms. Goodness knows, they are many and multifarious, devoted not just to tomatoes and tobacco but to a huge array of garden crops, shrubs, deciduous trees, and conifers. From grapes to hydrangeas and honeysuckle, catalpas to cayenne peppers, nothing in the plant kingdom is safe. The caterpillars of most species come equipped with dorsal horns at the end of the abdomen; the others sport only a token bump or show no protrusion at all. Most pupate in the ground; a few, however, spin their cocoons amid leaf litter. The zoological family to which they all belong, horned or not, comprises no fewer than 124 species, which are hardly confined to the Americas. One species is endemic to the fabled Galápagos. Another is mentioned in the Hippocratic medical literature of ancient Greece, in which instructions are given for concocting a remedy for a suppurating womb from the dried and pulverized *kampai* of the *tithumallis*—the caterpillars of the spurge hawk moth.

Tobacco Hornworm (*Manduca sexta*)

These spurge-devouring caterpillars are described as wearing a *ken-tron*—a spike on their rumps, and that's the clue to their identity.

But ugly though I find hornworms, I can hardly deny my fascination with the colors and patterns on their bodies. And if I were still smoking, I might even envy the tobacco hornworm's gift for remaining unaffected by nicotine, which turns many human beings into raving addicts and kills most bugs when it's used as an insecticide. All the nicotine ingested by the tobacco glutton is simply, quickly excreted. But, oh, the bodies and habits of all hornworms are repulsive—the squishy obesity, the incessantly moving jaws. Their only challengers in the race for the most despicable larvae among North America members of the order Lepidoptera might be the native tent caterpillars that year-in, year-out infest wild cherry trees—but these larvae provide food for titmice and yellow-billed cuckoos, and their cocoons, with some persuasion, yield usable silk. Another contestant might be the larva of the gypsy moth, imported from Europe in the late 1860s as a silk moth; these caterpillars, polka-dotted with red and blue, wearing tufts of golden hair, produce no silk for commercial harvest—produce no good at all that I can see—but rather leave defoliated forests in their wake. As for hornworms, what good are they? Apart from the Hippocratic remedy, I know of only two benefits that they confer on humankind. The first involves only a single spike-tailed species, *Ceratomia catalpae*, the "hornworm of the catalpa tree." It is intentionally gathered up by anglers, turned inside out, and threaded onto a fishing hook as bait. The second is that entomologists find hornworms useful for research into matters like insect hormones and behavior; the caterpillars are large and easy to raise under laboratory conditions (nor has anyone ever complained about their maltreatment). But in the fashion of all successful creatures, hornworms care not a whit about being useful to anything other than themselves. No matter what the family, genus, and species, they and their creeping, crawling ilk are living proof of a primordial law: Whatever can be eaten, shall be. And yet, and yet—in the case of hornworms, ugliness and insatiability lead to something else, something that I gladly perceive as beauty. Metamorphosis works wonders in the hideous worm.

The family is that of the Sphingidae, the sphinxes. And the creature's caterpillar stage is responsible for the family's name, an ancient name that brings to mind pharaohs and pyramids, or Oedipus and riddles. The monumental Egyptian version—its lion-body recumbent and its regal head (thought to be that of the pharaoh Kafre) alert and upright—still guards the desert near Giza. But the Sphinx sent by the goddess Hera to punish the Greek city of Thebes has not been seen since the days of Oedipus. With a woman's head on a lion's body, the wings of an eagle, and a writhing, lashing snake for a tail, she crouched atop a mountain on the road to Thebes, barring the way to travelers. It was her habit to taunt all passersby with a riddle: What being with but one voice goes on four legs in the morning, two at noon, three in the evening, and is weakest when it has the most? She would most bloodily dispatch all those who failed to answer, and that was everyone until Oedipus, journeying toward Thebes to learn his fortunes from an oracle, was challenged but prevailed: Man, who crawls as a baby, walks upright as a youth, and leans upon a stick in his old age. Though it is not recorded, I think that the Sphinx must have screamed, must have shivered the air and set the mountain to trembling with her rage and disappointment. But it is known that she leaped from the mountain in defeat, and her broken corpse was found in the valley below.

It is, however, not her monstrosity (though perhaps it should have been) that led the classifiers of insects, men learned in classical studies as well as entomology, to take one gander at a typical horn-worm and promptly attach her name to the whole family. Rather, it is her posture, and that of her Egyptian counterpart. Head and thorax uplifted to appraise the world, abdomen stretched out flat behind, the sphinx caterpillar unwittingly mimics its namesake's pose. And, wonder of wonders, in those still moments it ceases chewing. But then the tireless jaws begin to scissor at the leaves again. Like cookie crumbs falling from a small child's mouth, bits of greenery drift to the ground. And if there are enough caterpillars at work, you can hear their droppings steadily bombarding the leaves below.

Yet the reason for this gross, obsessive appetite is transformation. Egg to larva, larva to pupa, pupa to adult, moth and butterfly retell an old tale: once again, the ugly duckling turns into a swan; once again, the frog becomes a prince. But the story of butterfly and moth occurs in real-world terms, which makes their onrolling transformations more marvelous than anything imagined in a fairy tale.

The adult sphinx moth is indeed a marvel. Ash sphinx, laurel sphinx, pawpaw sphinx—some have common names centered on their favorite food. Waved sphinx, one-eyed sphinx, clearwing, and five-spotted hawk moth (the tomato hornworm's apotheosis)—some are named for notable features of their appearance. Some names, like those of Carter's and Abbot's sphinxes, honor people, while places are mentioned in others—Canadian sphinx and Carolina sphinx (the elegant transfiguration of the lowly tobacco hornworm). Myth also figures—the Pluto sphinx, recalling the Roman god of the underworld, and the Nessus sphinx, named for the centaur whose burning blood was used to kill the hero Hercules. Still other names seem to consist of commentary—rustic, hermit, plebeian, and mournful sphinxes. All these moths, and the hundred others that I have not mentioned, are not just beautiful but in some measure astonishing. Their colors tend toward the conservative: blends of black, gray, and brown, often embellished with orange spots or patches. And the clearwings have no color at all in the center of their wings, which are scaleless and as transparent as a windowpane. A hummingbird clearwing visits the butterfly bush planted beside our front deck; true to its name, wings beating so fast that they're nearly invisible, it hovers above the flowers and sips the nectar with its long, long tongue. But in respects other than color, the sphinxes are spectacular indeed. Whatever their size—most are medium to large—they possess long, pointed wings that project from their plump, furry bodies like the elongated wings of a sailplane. With those wings, they sometimes attain a ground speed of thirty-five miles an hour, outflying most insects of any kind, including the other moths. Flight takes warmth; they contract their flight muscles until sufficient heat is generated to give their wings lift, and once airborne, they maintain a body temperature of 100 degrees Fahrenheit. Nor are their forays into the air fluttering and windblown; instead, maneuvering with exceeding strength and skill, they are able to rise vertically in the air and even to fly backward. The sphinxes may also be the least silent of moths. By inhaling and exhaling air, they can produce a chirp, which is the music of love, designed to attract a mate.

At the end of June, the green beans are done, with twenty-three pints put up and more given away. July brings fourteen pints of limas, which translate into eleven pounds of shelled beans. By the end of July, the tomato vines begin to give out, though not because of hornworm appetites; the falling yield is due rather to a month of fierce sun and little rain. But I have better than one hundred pints in the freezer and on the shelves—tomatoes stewed with onions and green peppers, tomatoes plus jalapeños, tomatoes with eggplant or in wine sauce, tomatoes canned plain, green tomato pickles, and sweet red tomato relish, along with juice, of course, and soup. The crop has been big enough to satisfy every comer, from orchard orioles to box turtles, from hornworms to woman. In mid-September, putting the garden to bed, the Chief begins with removal of tomato cages and stakes.

"Hon," he calls, "come look!" Inside fixing lunch, I'm galvanized by his urgent tone. He stands by the steps to the back deck, a tomato stake in his hand. On the stake rests a moth. The wings, folded over its body and patterned in the subtlest shades of brown, beige, and charcoal gray, look newly dry. The moth has emerged from the underworld only this morning. When at last it flies, the orange spots on its abdomen show clear: *M. sexta*, Carolina sphinx, scourge of the Chief's tobacco-cropping days. It lands three feet away on the trunk of a loblolly pine, where it is camouflaged by the barklike appearance of its wings.

That instant, my mind rewords the riddle of the Sphinx: What being sleeps at dawn, crawls at noon, then sleeps again but wakes in the evening to winged flight?

Carolina Sphinx (*Manduca sexta*)

LEGS

Garden Centipede *(Scolopendrid sp.)*

Centipedes

"THERE I was, sixteen years old, in the little basement apartment my dad had built for me. And there *it* was, a centipede, just a-gittin' it across the wall. I hit it with a phone book. It came in two—one teeny piece and the other with all those legs that kept moving and moving." Laura shudders. "Eew, that did it!"

Laura, wife of my elder son, is a down-to-earth woman, good at mothering and growing flowers. She's not usually fazed by anything that creeps or crawls, slithers, bites, or stings—except for centipedes. That apparition on her wall, that invasion of her space and her sensibilities, might well have been foreseen, however, had anyone been thinking at the outset of the preferred habitat of these small, swift, many-legged animals. The apartment, consisting of a tiny living room and bedroom, was ideally damp and dark. Laura's father had thought of pleasing her, while Laura, being the age she was, had mostly considered her newly acquired ease in sneaking out.

But those legs, those remarkable, multiple legs—she's brought up an interesting point. It occurs to me to wonder just how a centipede can move without treading on its own toes and tripping all over itself. As an old ditty has it:

> The centipede was happy quite
>   Until a toad in fun
> Said, "Pray, which leg comes after which?"
> That worked her mind to such a pitch,
> She lay distracted in a ditch
>   Considering how to run.

Surely, any other means of locomotion would be more efficient, from the snake's no legs to the spider's eight. More than eight legs seem a nonsensical abundance or, worse, a repulsive superfluity. Yet centipedes thrive, and so do millipedes with an even greater number of legs (where centipedes have one pair of legs per segment, millipedes have two and can also curl themselves into a tight little spiral). And there is an ever-scurrying host of other similarly overen-

Millipede (*Parajulus impressus*)

dowed, like horseshoe crabs and the tiny centipedelike pauropods with eight to ten pairs of stumpy legs.

All of these belong to the kingdom of the Animalia and to its most populous subdivision, the phylum Arthropoda, the "joint-legged" animals. Insects in their uncountable legions are arthropods. So are the crustaceans—"shell creatures"—like the barnacles, blue crabs, and shrimp found in my underwater front yard in North Carolina; the chelicerates, or "horny claws," which include both horseshoe crabs and the many arachnids—spiders, ticks, chiggers, mites, and scorpions; the trilobites—"three-lobed creatures"—now extinct, that swarmed in Cambrian seas 450 million years ago; and the uniramians—"one branchers"—a subphylum that gathers in several classes of terrestrial animals, among them the six-legged insects, or hexapods, and the mob of Myriapoda, which means "ten thousand–leggers." (Whoever named the myriapods—and this large group's "hundred-legger" centipedes, its "thousand-legger" millipedes—may easily be forgiven repeated exaggeration: the legs of these animals are often the first thing noticed. And there is a European species of centipede that has committed an anatomical exaggeration all on its own: it sports no fewer than 177 pairs of legs.)

"One brancher" may seem a curious term. But it means that the uniramians have one limb, and only one, extending from each possible location, while the biramous marine arthropods—the crustaceans, horseshoe crabs, long-lost trilobites, and others—have two, one of which is easily recognizable as a limb, while its partner is feathery and gill-like. The two-branched animals inhabit the fossil record almost as far back as it goes, but not the one-branched kind. So it is reasonably thought that, long ago, the arthropods evolved and diversified on land after a group of soft-bodied marine animals with somewhat hardened heads had left the sea behind forever, and taken up residence amid the heavy vegetation of coastal wetlands. They may have crept ashore on lobopods, or lobe legs, which are highly variable knoblets of flesh able to be extended or retracted; a set of lobopods near the head—future mandibles—would have been used to spoon food into the mouth. The first requirements of these creatures, the needs that shaped their evolution, were to shield themselves from both water and air, the former lest their bodies absorb a chemically imbalancing amount of freshwater, the latter lest they dry out completely in the seaside breezes. And they had to find food. Their legs developed sections, from the coxa, which is closest to the body, on through the trochanter, femur, and tibia to the often many-jointed tarsus; some joints swung like hinges and other like pivots. Their skins turned into armor—an exoskeleton of hardened cuticle that protected the animals' soft innards. The ancestors of flies and moths grew wings and flew; the aboriginal spiders and myriapods opted for a plenitude of legs and good ground speed, while the protograsshoppers and crickets developed a sturdy third pair of legs that gave great jumping power; still other land-going arthropods evolved an ability to sting or to curl into a defensive ball. Some reached adulthood though metamorphosis, while others hatched out as miniature versions of the grown-up arthropod and attained greater size through successive molts. But whatever routes they took, they thrived—the fossil record (for what it's worth) shows no massive extinctions—and became the present multitude of uniramous animals: the insects, the myriapods, and the minuscule pauropods and their close cousins the symphalids.

Of them all, the centipedes are indeed a mighty crew. Ranging the world, they tally in at about twenty-eight hundred species and warrant a myriapod class of their very own, the Chilopoda—the "jaw-leggers." That class is in turn divided into two subclasses, the

Epimorpha, "whole shapes," which hatch complete with every one of their many adult segments, and the Anamorpha, the "growing shapes," which hatch without the full complement but gain segments as they molt. These subclasses are each further divided into two orders with wonderfully descriptive names. The epimorphic kinds, both short-legged, are, first, the Geophilida, the reclusive "earth lovers," or soil centipedes with 31 to 177 pairs of legs, that burrow into the ground in the fashion of earthworms, and, second, the Scolopendrida, the "millipedes," so named because of their superficial resemblance to true millipedes—the dark dorsal surface and all those legs, legs, legs, from 21 to 33 pairs, depending on the species. The scolopendrids, sometimes called garden centipedes, are a primarily tropical group that in its largest incarnations reaches nearly a foot in length. The anamorphs, which never attain such a truly monstrous size, consist of the Lithobiida, the "stone" centipedes often found under rocks, and the Scutigerida, the "shield bearers," named for the hardened scutes, or plates, on their backs. The shield bearers, commonly known as house centipedes, are the critters with superlong, spidery legs that haunt sinks and bathtubs and run like speed demons across damp basement walls like Laura's. But no matter to which family they belong, centipedes are primarily nocturnal. All of them prefer to hang out in dim, dank places, like rotting logs, leaf mold, moist soil, or drains. All are predators; all are fiercely dedicated carnivores.

It is their method of catching prey that has awarded them the name of jaw-leggers. The pair of jointed limbs on the first body segment after the head have become modified into poison claws, sometimes called poison jaws (the technical term is toxicognaths) that inject a paralyzing venom into hapless victims, like worms or arthropods of other species. These claws are never used for locomotion but are held so closely under the mouthparts that they appear to be part of the animal's eating apparatus. Which indeed they are, for the poison they pump out is used for external digestion; it works not just to stun prey but helps to break down its soft tissues. Peculiarly, the choices of prey and eating habits are not the same with anamorphs and epimorphs. The latter, all short-legged, and some as short-sighted as Mr. Magoo but most of them completely blind, seek their dinners in confined, night-dark places like subterranean crevices and the undersides of decaying logs. They don't, however, need to see in the dark. Other senses and abilities help them out. While the scolopendrids skitter and wriggle into the merest crannies, the soil centipedes thicken segments of their bodies in earthworm fashion to exert a strong thrust forward and thus move through the earth in search of prey. It has been said that, blind as they are, both kinds of epimorphs must "stumble on food by accident." When it has been found (by accident or by intent), they swallow it whole if it is small or use their strong and hefty poison claws to paralyze and tear holes in larger prey, then insert their heads to suck up the soft parts. One large scolopendrid, *Craterostigmus tasmanianus*, which has some eyesight and is native to Tasmania and New Zealand, has been observed using its poison claws to pull termites out of cracks and to drill tunnels through compacted decaying wood. The long-legged anamorphs pursue another way of hunting. They look for prey with capture aforethought and are able to deal with tougher, harder food. The little stone centipede is particularly good at weaseling into crevices but without thrusting or pushing as the geophilids do. The house centipede, *Scutigera coleoptrata*, is surely the mightiest hunter of all the chilopods. (Its genus is "shield bearer," but the species name, bestowed by the master taxonomist Linnaeus himself, seems to mean "sheath wings," perhaps because its body, like a beetle's, appears to be sheathed. That's only a guess, for the name makes no good classical sense; nor can we wake Linnaeus to find out what he meant.) The house centipede is blessed with excellent vision; it works in more open places and can spot a fly or a spider before the victim is aware of impending doom. And in the chase, the creature runs like a greyhound, attaining top speeds in an instant. This kind of swiftness leads to great success in pouncing on and stunning normally wary food creatures like cockroaches and

flies. The poison claws of the anamorphs are small and light compared to those of their epimorphic cousins, but their large, powerful
mandibles can cut well-armored food like a beetle into pieces small
enough for swallowing.

I hear the question rising: What hurt can a creature with poison claws put on a human being? The answer is, Not anything you'd
notice much—unless, that is, you were seized and injected by one
of the tropical models nearly a foot long. Even then, the bite,
though uncomfortable, would hardly be fatal. Some scolopendrids
can also use the hindmost pair of legs to pinch, but such an attack
would produce more fright than pain. Our kind, however, is not
irrationally averse to the very notion of pinches and venomous
claws (not to mention the frisson raised by the skitter and scurry).

Centipedes do, however, have their human uses. We have managed to render the word *centipede* impotent by detaching the name
from the animal and applying it both to a lawn grass, much favored
in the South, that sends out fine-textured runners and grows so
densely that it shuts out weeds, and to a computer game in which
creepy-crawlies invade a mushroom patch. (That game is surely a
way of transforming computer "bugs" from objects of frustration to
subjects of fun.) And the people of Silver City, New Mexico, featured various contests as part of their annual Mining Days festival,
which was discontinued, alas, in the mid-1990s. Prizes were
awarded to the people fielding the fastest, heaviest, longest, and
best-dressed hundred-leggers. Yes, like the star performers in a flea
circus, some entrants wore costumes. Why centipedes? As one former resident puts it, "Little desert towns have to think of something
to celebrate."

Nonetheless, an unexpected sight of the real thing can be off-
putting, to say the least. I confess to being utterly unnerved, to
flinching and yelping when I settled down on the sofa one chilly
evening to read, reached for my favorite throw, and found a motion-
less centipede snuggled therein. Not the long-legged sink-and-tub
kind but a dark, short-legged sort, which I immediately shook onto

the floor—and almost as immediately regretted not having observed. The sharp eyes of my husband, the Chief, found it half an hour later. It had traveled thirty feet from the living room well into the hall. Becoming brave, I tweezered it, put it in a small jar with alcohol, and later sent it to the entomologists at North Carolina State University. Behold: a juvenile scolopendrid—*Hemiscolopendra punctiventris*, to be exact. (The name, a fine example of taxonomical, not classical, Greco-Latin, means "point-bellied half-millipede.") Along with the identification, the entomologists sent a detailed note: "This particular species is native to North Carolina and is commonly found in woodland areas. Our dry weather has sent many insects and other critters, such as millipedes, indoors in search of moisture, and it is likely that the centipede entered the house in search of prey." Then, with the assumption (natural but quite mistaken) that I had sent in the specimen because I wanted mainly to know how to commit acts of extermination, the note concludes: "Since only one specimen was found, you have solved the problem. Spraying is not really necessary, since these incidences are usually sporadic, and it is difficult (often impossible) to target specific areas to treat indoors." But within days of finding the first, I came across two more indoor point-bellies, one alive, the other completely dessicated. And though there's still an involuntary flinch when one makes a sudden appearance, I'm more interested in counting their legs. *H. punctiventris* boasts twenty pairs plus one—the concealed poison claws.

Flinch factor aside, a few things may be said in favor of centipedes. They do, for example, exhibit family feeling. The scolopendrids guard their eggs until they hatch; females curl around them and may even lick them on occasion, supposedly to keep them clean. There also seems to be some parent-offspring communication in all the chilopod orders. Centipedes may also serve as objects of pity, for they are not always the winners in the eat-or-be-eaten game. One species of ant, *Amblyopone pallipes*, for example, has a taste for hundred-leggers, but because this kind of prey is often far too large to lug home, A. *pallipes* moves its larvae to their dinners. Centipedes are not without defenses. The little stone centipedes, for example, throw out sticky threads from their posterior legs to entangle predators like ants and wolf spiders. And silken strands are spun out by the male centipedes of some species to guide the females to their spermatophores, or sperm packages. Sex among these centipedes is not a matter of penetration but rather one of pick up and insert.

What you really want to know, if you're still with me, is how they run. Question: What goes ninety-nine, thump, ninety-nine, thump? Answer: a centipede with a wooden leg. Only a human being could construct that joke—or this one: If the first fifty legs of a centipede are going forty miles an hour, what are the last fifty doing? Hauling ass. The centipede has no interest, of course, in such frivolity. It lives to run and runs to live.

Just how it runs is a matter that has received considerable study. Centipedes of every family have been kept in laboratories, where, alive, they are incited to thicken their segments or do high kicks for photographs and to scurry across smoked paper, leaving telltale patterns of footprints as they go; where, dead, they are dissected and subjected to microscopic examinations of their most intimate anatomical details, from their brains and digestive systems to the muscles in their bodies and legs. In that last department, it has been discovered that the animals are particularly well equipped with intrinsic (in-leg) and extrinsic (in-body) muscles affecting their locomotion. Each of these muscles tends to several tasks: flexing, lifting, lowering, or rotating the appendage to which it is attached. (The rotation is an action to which science has given the term "leg rocking"; it helps position a leg for the best push forward.) The geophilids are the pikers in the muscle department, with only thirteen extrinsic muscles for each leg, but multiply that thirteen by forty legs—the grand total is 520. The scolopendrids achieve a somewhat higher count at nineteen extrinsic muscles for each leg, and the stone centipedes boast twenty. The champs, however, are the scutigerids, with an amazing thirty-four each. The difference explains why the scutigerids get out of the starting gate so fast, while the epimorphic species, less amply endowed, need to start off slowly and shift up to speed. But the mere fact that each of the many legs is fitted out with a boggling number of muscles does not in itself explain how the animals manage not to trip themselves. As big centipede says to little centipede in a 1998 *Wall Street Journal* cartoon, "Strength and speed are useful, son, but coordination is *crucial.*"

Imagine a chorus line. Imagine the Rockettes or a ruffled flurry of cancan dancers or a troupe of high-kicking showgirls in Las Vegas. The main difference is that while the line is composed of separate entities acting as one, the centipede's parts are all irredeemably attached one to another. Then, while a chorus line may specialize in synchronous movements, its members stepping uniformly in the same direction at the same time, the centipede runs with undulating leg movements known as metachronal rhythms. The legs do not work in unison but rather in succession. At low speeds pairs of legs operate in the same fashion, but in an all-out dash, they each take on different roles, with some on the ground, others in the air. At any given moment, some legs perform the propulsive backstroke that pushes the animal forward, while others lift off the ground, stretch out, and swing in preparation for their turn at pushing. A centipede runs, says one researcher, "by a series of gaits in which the phase difference between successive legs and the relative duration of the forward and backward strokes by the leg change harmoniously." The gaits depend, that is, on which legs are moving and for how long they lift or push. These movements look something like grass rippling beneath a breeze. But all centipedes run with immense precision. The tracks recorded on smoked paper show distinctive patterns for various species, with successive footprints often being placed on the one same spot. In their fastest mode, the scolopendrids, which tend to weave a bit from side to side as they run, use only three legs at one time for propulsion, while the other thirty-seven move through the air. The stone and house centipedes, many of which which have only fourteen pairs of legs to run with, fly straight ahead like arrows. The longer the legs, the longer the stride of an animal, and the greater its speed. And some amazing speeds have been recorded in the laboratory, with *S. coleoptrata*, the house centipede, clocking in at more than sixteen inches per second, though it is thought to run much faster in the wild.

The leg movements that Laura saw, however, were chaotic, inspired by the involuntary muscular contractions that occur after death. I hope that I can convince her, as I've convinced myself by looking into their lives and habits, that centipedes, all unaware, are full of grace. Aside from which, they eat cockroaches.

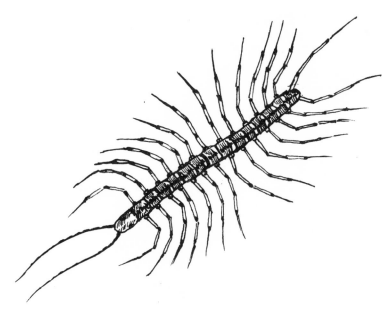

House Centipede (*Scutigera coleoptrata*)

HERITAGE

Kudzu *(Pueraria montana)* on Cabin

Kudzu

"**G**OATS do a pretty good job," says the cooperative extension agent. He goes on to recommend a popular herbicide in case I don't have a goat.

I've just asked him how kudzu, that perennial and extraordinarily aggressive vine, is best kept within bounds. In a sense, my question is rhetorical, for none of the stuff grows on the riverside land that my husband, the Chief, and I call home during the balmier months of the year. But in another sense, it's not. Go a mile or two inland: there, with lush exuberance, the vine has seized many unfarmed portions of the landscape.

Throughout the South, kudzu creeps with stealthy swiftness over brushpiles and fences. It climbs trees and telephone poles and casts its soft but heavy net over thickets and hedgerows. It enshrouds abandoned houses, tumbledown tobacco barns, rusted appliances, and junked cars. It sneaks into gardens and plowed fields. Displacing innocent native vegetation, it twines, curls, shoots upward and outward with relentless green insistence. In its wake, power outages occur, and trains have been derailed. By the mid-1990s, kudzu had laid claim to more than 7,000,000 acres—almost 11,000 square miles—of the South. Monstrous roots thrust deep into the earth of at least sixteen states, ropey vines embrace the landscape, and leaves smother it in a big, soft, fuzzy, unbreakable hug. Once the vine invades any location, getting rid of it is well nigh impossible. And it seizes another 120,000 acres every year, a rate that can only increase with the increase in the plant's domain.

Only a decade-long drenching with herbicide could end such a massive takeover—if, that is, the anti-kudzu factor of the population, and that's almost everyone, could be rallied into a concerted effort. (A more important consideration for many of us might be the degree of comfort we feel about using manufactured herbicides in the first place.) As for goats, I doubt that the world has enough of them to eat their way to a solution of the problem.

Kudzu *is* a problem. Not only are fortunes in private and public money spent annually on its control and eradication, but the vine is rude enough to affront human sensibilities; unruly, running wild, operating only by genetically encoded instructions, it defeats our every attempt to assert our superiority. It's vegetation with a vengeance, a sprawling, mindless, inordinately grabby menace. Or, as my Southern-speaking friends and neighbors have put it, the damned stuff's a right sorry mess.

Yet, it has virtues. Without them, it wouldn't have spread so far so fast.

Kudzu came to America by invitation more than a century ago. Now it has moved in, the very model of a sorner—a guest, that is, who overstays the initial welcome, becomes entrenched, and places undue burdens on an unwilling but helpless host. Yet this native of the Far East was escorted here with much praise for its beauty and usefulness. And it is an attractive plant. The young vines are tender, the more mature vines, woody. The deciduous leaves, sometimes entire but usually lobed, grow in groups of three on softly hairy stems; each one is as big as my hand. The leaves, along with the young vines, provide certifiably nutritious fodder for livestock. The densely clustered flowers, purple as Concord grapes and just as fragrant, bloom in late summer. With the onset of cold weather, the leaves are shed and top growth dies back, leaving dry, sticklike tangles. The fuzzy brown seedpods look something like woolly bear caterpillars. The plant, however, rarely produces itself by seeds, which resist sprouting unless the hard seed coverings have been scarified—that is, softened or cut. The alacrity of its spread is accounted for partly by the fifty- to one-hundred-foot growth of the vines each season—more than a foot a day—and by its habit of sending down roots whenever a leaf node touches the ground. These root crowns, like those of ivy, easily produce new plants. But when a seed manages to sprout and the resulting vine does not lie on the ground but shoots aloft, climbing a fence, a tree, or a telephone pole, the resultant root develops massive proportions. Old roots have tapped as deeply as twelve feet into the ground and may weigh anywhere from two hundred to four hundred pounds.

The Japanese, who make an edible starch from the roots, are usually given full credit for kudzu's introduction. Its very name is an Americanization of *kuzu*, the Japanese word for the plant. It was they who exhibited this country's first living, growing specimen in their pavilion at the Philadelphia Centennial Exposition, which opened in May, 1876, and they showed it again in 1883 at the New Orleans Exposition. The Japanese, however, were not entirely responsible for kudzu's entry and all the ensuing complications. An American was involved, one Thomas Hogg (1820–1892), who had been sent to Japan in 1862 at the behest of none other than President Abraham Lincoln, and there, for the next eight years, he filled the post of United States marshal. Toward the end of his tenure, he worked closely with the Japanese customs service and, in 1872, returned at the Japanese government's request to continue this work for another two years.

I came, I saw, I picked it up and brought it home—this might be a guiding principle for many travelers, known and unknown. Their ranks include Marco Polo, Columbus, Cortés and de Soto, Captain John Smith, Captain James Cook, and Charles Darwin. As they sailed the seven seas or slogged through the New World, they collected everything that had ignited their admiration, beckoned to their greed, or simply tickled their curiosity. And what a hodge-podge the collections were—goods and curiosa that ranged from spices and gold to lizards, raccoons, and sassafras trees. Japan came late into the scrutiny of the Western world, but when the country was at last opened to foreigners in the mid-1800s, a good many of the Europeans and Americans who went there followed the grand, acquisitive example of earlier travelers. And how could the Honorable Mr. Hogg resist? The son of a noted horticulturist who ran a nursery business in New York, he had learned botany in his cradle days. Later, the decade of service in Japan provided him with ample time in which to indulge his passion for plants and also send home many specimens that had caught his fancy. He sent them on their transpacific journey in a recently designed container called a Wardian case, after its inventor Nathaniel B. Ward; it was a sealed terrarium with a glass dome set atop a sturdy wooden box filled with soil in which the plants had already taken root. Some of the plants that Thomas Hogg introduced into the United States are popular today, among them the katsura tree (*Cercidiphyllum japonicum,* "Japanese tree with leaves shaped like a weaver's shuttle") and, especially, Japanese stewartia (*Stewartia pseudocamellia,* "Stewart's false camellia"), with its exfoliating mauve and silver bark and its huge flowers comprising five snowy petals around an orange-gold central disk. But stewartia's popularity is deserved; it's a well-behaved plant, possessed of the good manners that kudzu sadly lacks.

Yet on its home ground in the Far East, kudzu has ever observed the proprieties. Climate and native pests help keep it in check, along with its regular harvest for a host of human uses. (I think it likely that its spread in densely populated Japan is also limited by the need to make the most efficient use of available land.) The plant is assigned to the genus *Pueraria,* which is divided, depending on the source used, into anywhere from ten to fifteen species, originating variously in China, Japan, Taiwan, or India. *Pueraria* seems a classically Latinate designation—except that it yields no meaning when I consult a lexicon. I consult a friend instead, the poet Jeffery Beam, who is most fortuitously employed in the botany section of a noted university's biology library. He finds that the name has nothing to do with Latin, nor is it connected with anything Oriental. Rather, Switzerland's Augustin Pyramus de Candolle (1778–1841), one of the truly great nineteenth-century botanists and a member of an important botanical family, named it for his compatriot and fellow plantsman Marc Nicolas Puerari (1776–1845), who had donated his private herbarium—his collection of dried and systematically arranged specimens—to the family. M. de Candolle bestowed the generic name no later than 1825, the year that *Pueraria,* according to the custom of the time, received a sumptuous description in Latin. Just how he and

Puerari came across kudzu in the first place remains a secret, but it's surely safe to think that some European traveler, impelled (like Marco Polo and Thomas Hogg) by collector's fever, saw it, picked it up, and brought it home.

The vine that has thrust its roots deep down into U.S. soil is *P. montana*, "mountain kudzu," which was known until very recently as *P. lobata*, "lobed kudzu" (botanical nomenclature, like that for all other living things, undergoes cyclic upheavals). But the American venture was by no means *P. montana*'s first move into a foreign land; native to China, it was brought into Japan no later than the sixth century A.D., and there it quickly, contentedly settled in, appearing not only as a feature of the landscape but also as an ingredient in recipes, an item in the natural pharmacopoeia, and a subject for poems.

Every kudzu, of whatever species, belongs to the Leguminosae, the pea family, which comprises a stunning diversity of flowers, shrubs, vines, and trees, all of which produce seeds contained in pods. The snap peas growing in our spring garden, the green beans we've yet to plant are both kin to kudzu, as is the soy that will be harvested, come September, in the fields of nearby farms. Also part of this huge family are the various clovers and the spurred butterfly pea, a delicate lavender-colored wildflower, that rejoice in our seldom-mowed yard. So are the tough-rooted plants called devil's shoestring that my brothers grubbed out of the pastures on my father's farm, the trefoils with seeds that stick tight as ticks to my socks, and the poisonous locoweeds of the Midwest, not to mention the gentler bluebonnet, pride of Texas. And so are shrubs like broom and woody, climbing vines like wisteria, along with orna-mental trees—acacia, redbud, mimosa, honey locust, and a host of flowering, sweet-smelling others. Except for the frozen polar deserts, no part of the world lacks members of the family.

Kudzu's arrival in America may have been predestined. Even without Thomas Hogg and the showcasing of the plant at the Japanese exhibits in 1876 and 1883, it would have made its way to the New World for both aesthetic and culinary reasons, and also, it's likely, for its amazing, colossal, downright stupendous habits of growth (Americans have ever been enamored of wonders, freaks, and marvels, indeed of all manifestations of the biggest, the best, the least, the worst, and similar extremes). But its entry, though thoroughly triumphal, was accomplished with little fanfare, and the plant's initial popularity was based on its leafy beauty and the friendly shade it could cast on porches that would otherwise bake and swelter in the direct rays of the sun. For more than fifty years, from its introduction into the 1930s, kudzu seemed a benign, quite amiable alternative to the bee-rich grapevines, climbing red roses, twining blue morning glories, and other greenery often planted by porchside trellises to moderate the fierceness of the summer sun.

The story of kudzu's takeover is an oft-told tale that has been featured in many publications, from agricultural bulletins and forestry magazines to the front page of the *Wall Street Journal*. At least two books have been devoted to its history and real or putative uses. Suffice it here to summarize the events that led to the transformation of an ornamental plant known fondly as the "porch vine" into the apparently limitless, all-devouring vegetative sprawl that has entered folk parlance as the "vine that ate the South."

Although there were signs early on that kudzu had an appetite for escape and an unquenchable zest for proliferation, its partisans by far outnumbered the monitory skeptics until the early 1950s, a full seventy-five years after it had begun to snuggle itself firmly and probably forever into the South. Some who issued warnings were farmers who refused to let kudzu set one tendril, one rooting leaf node on their land. Today, their names have disappeared into the crevices of history. One name that survives, however, is that of David Fairchild, who worked before the turn of the century as a plant explorer, seeking useful specimens abroad, for the U.S. Department of Agriculture and in the early 1900s became the department's chief. In that capacity, he'd served in Japan, where his eye, like that of Thomas Hogg, had alighted on wild kudzu; his interest, however, was centered not on the plant's beauty but rather on its undeniable appeal to grazing and browsing animals and its high nutritive value. So he brought it along when he came back home. His particular misadventure happened in his own yard in Washington, D.C., where he'd set in seedlings. And there his vines grew quickly into luxuriant specimens that had a tendency to emulate Pinocchio: he'd planted kudzu, given it a good home, but it ran away. It covered his shrubs, climbed his trees, and made of itself "an awful tangled nuisance." This description, along with advice to exercise great caution, appears in his book *The World Was My Garden: Travels of a Plant Explorer,* which was written in 1902 but not published until 1938. By then, it was much too late for his warnings to bring the runaway back into even a semblance of domesticity.

But by the turn of the century, when David Fairchild first discovered kudzu's potential for trouble, others in both private and public life were promoting its virtues with the intensity and fervor of true believers. In their vanguard were Charles and Lillie Pleas, Quakers and dedicated conservationists, who had moved in the early 1900s to Chipley, Florida. There they not only promoted kudzu as a superior forage crop and the best-ever means to control erosion but also established a commercial nursery, which propagated the vine from seeds, cuttings, and root crowns and sold it well into the 1940s. On the outskirts of Chipley, a bronze historical marker, surmounted by the state seal of Florida, now honors their efforts: KUDZU DEVELOPED HERE.

But the Pleases' earnest and unceasing dedication centered on practical uses for the wonder plant. The work of Channing Cope took another form; it was a carnival of hype and hucksterism. From the late 1930s to the end of the 1940s, styling himself the Father of Kudzu and the Kudzu King, he extolled the virtues of the vine, writing often in the *Atlanta Journal-Constitution* and delivering a daily radio broadcast from the front porch of his house at Yellow River Farm. When he'd purchased the old farm near Atlanta, it had consisted of seven hundred eroded, unproductive acres, but kudzu, which he set in to improve the soil and serve as pasturage for cattle, worked its thickety green magic almost overnight. As possessed as a pearly-gates preacher by joyful certitude, he not only used his pulpits in the media to promote the vine's cause but also founded the Kudzu Club of America. With meetings, contests to see who could plant the most kudzu, and the election of kudzu queens, the club at its peak boasted twenty thousand members. But after Cope died in 1962, his dreams withered on the vine by the chill of disfavor, the kudzu he'd planted on Yellow River Farm overran the house from which he'd made his broadcasts and pulled it to the ground. To this day, however, the *Journal-Constitution* runs features on kudzu that grant the stuff a sort of quizzical praise, and towns in Georgia, Alabama, and Mississippi regularly hold kudzu festivals—all of which just goes to show that a bane serves as well as a blessing in giving folks an excuse to eat, drink, and make merry.

Channing Cope, however, leaped aboard the kudzu wagon well after it had picked up steam. Nor was it private efforts, like his and those of the Pleases, that caused a tidal surge of greenery to inundate the South. Credit—or blame, as the case may be—lies with the federal government and, more particularly, with Franklin Roosevelt's New Deal. In 1933, Congress brought into being the Soil Erosion Service, which two years later became the Soil Conservation Service (SCS), the name under which it operates today. In one tidy bundle, the work of the SCS addressed two of the major problems of the Depression era: the high unemployment rate and the rapidly failing productivity of Southern soil, which had been eroded and leached to exhaustion by two hundred years of farming methods that reaped crops but did not replace the nutrients needed to grow them. Enter the Civilian Conservation Corps (CCC), which aimed to keep young, unmarried men off the streets and out of bread lines by putting them to work at many soil-saving projects, from building flood-control levees to planting kudzu throughout the South. The U.S. Department of Agriculture published promotional literature on the vine, which could indeed keep worn-out farmland from washing away because it readily took hold in soil too poor to support anything else. The government not only established nurseries but also coaxed farmers into planting root-crowns and seedlings (some of the latter imported from Japan) by offering a cash incentive of up to eight dollars an acre—a fortune in those hard times. And once kudzu was on a roll, no one could stop its forward drive.

"We've got this concern that you're going to incriminate us or our agency," Bobby says in mock terror. Then he implores me, "Be kind to us, please."

Bobby is Robert Whitescarver, a slim, wiry man in his early forties who works for the SCS as a Natural Resources Team Leader for three large administrative units in the western part of Virginia. He's headquartered in Augusta County, my home territory, which lies in the center of the Shenandoah Valley; it's bounded by the Blue Ridge on the east and on the west by Great North Mountain, part of the long, lean Western Range of the Appalachians.

It's not kudzu country, or not in any worrisome way. The only place that I've seen it growing was along the back-yard fence of the house in which, two decades ago, I occupied the basement apartment. At that time, acquainted with the plant only by scowling rumor, I'd thought that the large-leafed vine winding itself around the fence wires was a watermelon, a volunteer that had sprouted, as they do, from a seed *thhhped* out by someone (perhaps me) on a hot summer day. Not a bad-looking plant. A rather decorative plant, in fact, and one that could perform a service by covering the naked fence wires. But a clue to its identity soon came along: the vine showed an extraordinary capacity for growth; indeed, it leaped forward several inches every night. Strip off the leaves, rip out the young root—I showed no mercy. It did not return the next year.

Bobby says that kudzu's not a problem in the valley—too cold—and that little of it was planted there in the 1930s and 1940s, the years that the SCS promoted it, propagated it, and set it ineradicably into tens of thousands of acres in the South. With him, however, is the man he calls an "angel of the conservation movement." This particular angel, gray-haired, somewhat rotund, and blessed with a smile as ample as the whole outdoors, is retired District Conservationist Wayne Hypes, who admits to planting some kudzu in the valley—"not much, though, not much." In his soft Southern voice, the word comes out as "plainting."

"I know your mother, go to the same church," Wayne says, introducing himself in Southern fashion, which aims to establish connections wherever possible. And he tells me that it was he who designed and supervised the construction of the small stream-fed lake on my father's Augusta County farm forty years ago. (The lake was stocked with bream and smallmouth bass; their descendants may be caught today.) Only then does he embark on his tale of service with the SCS. Now seventy-eight years old, he well remembers kudzu's glory days. In 1941, when he was twenty, he joined the SCS and was sent forthwith as a soil conservationist to the CCC camp in Mocksville, North Carolina, just southwest of Winston-Salem. He describes the work done by the members of the corps: "The first thing I saw them do was to construct terraces to cut down erosion on cotton land and tobacco land, and the next thing I saw them do was to plaint kudzu to heal up gullies." Then, as their supervisor, he determined where they should terrace and where set in cuttings. In November of 1941, he turned twenty-one; in February 1942, three months after the Japanese attack on Pearl Harbor, he reported to the Army and was subsequently sent to the South Pacific. Nor did he leave kudzu behind. There he participated in the invasion of Morotai, an island located just north of the equator about midway between the Philippines and New Guinea. Once ashore, his company was assigned to dig anti-aircraft guns into the ground, build a berm around them, and camouflage them from enemy planes. Noticing wild kudzu everywhere and recalling its phenomenally rapid rate of growth, he bade his men did up some plants and set them on the berm of the gun emplacements. He remembers that "it grew so fast our guns were completely camouflaged in just a few days." After the war, in 1946, he was back in North Carolina, where little had changed on the SCS front: "They were still plainting kudzu and building terraces."

Then I learn one reason that Bobby has granted Wayne Hypes the status of an angel. With some bemusement, as if he's still shaking his head at being tapped back then by serendipity, Wayne says, "I was one of the first—and I'm proud of this, though I don't know where I got the idea—I laid out contour strips in Richmond County in North Carolina, the town of Rockingham. They'd never heard of those before. They were all using terraces." He adds that he also laid out some contour strips on my father's farm. He's talking about the practice, now standard, of leaving the land as is and planting along with its natural elevations and declivities to maximize soil retention and minimize erosion, rather than bringing in manpower and machines to work a sometimes brutal reshaping. The use of contour strips may have saved more farmland than any other method. Nonetheless, terrace or contour strip, the mission of SCS was to cover every inch with kudzu. In 1947, Wayne was transferred to Virginia, where the vine had already become well entrenched east of the Blue Ridge. He comments on the kudzu that covers the roadsides along Route 29 from Culpepper down to Danville. It's truly abundant there—lush, rank, and powerful. Rearing up trees and poles, it turns them into long-necked, leafy-headed brontosauruses, browsing in the great fields of the sky. The sight is somehow beautiful.

Wayne and Bobby both comment on other takeover plants. Kudzu is not the only exotic that has made a successful landgrab. Bobby notes somewhat ruefully that the SCS also raised cuttings and gave enthusiastic support to the planting of the multiflora rose (*Rosa multiflora*, the "many-flowered rose") as a living fence. Like kudzu it was imported from Asia in the nineteenth century as an ornamental plant. It puts on a lush display of small, fragrant white blossoms in the spring and in the fall bears red hips that are immensely attractive to wildlife, especially birds. And this species lived a tame, unobtrusive life in yards and gardens until the 1930s, when some of its other gifts—a kudzulike ability to flourish in poor soil and stabilize it, a habit of dense growth that could form windbreaks—came to federal attention. According to the wisdom of the time, multiflora rose would not spread on its own, for a seed fallen to earth could not sprout without prior scarification. But multiflora ran out of control, nor could anyone, not the SCS nor farmers who'd only wanted a living fence, call the renegade back. Birds, delighting in the fruit, performed the act of scarification in their digestive tracts: behold, multiflora throughout the eastern U.S., invading pastures and blanketing roadsides. I see it in the flatlands of Virginia and the Carolinas; I see it beside the switchbacks on West Virginia's steep mountain roads. Recapture is out of the question. But unlike kudzu, which left behind its natural controls when it crossed the ocean, the renegade rose is subject to insect predation and mite-borne disease. Therein may lie hope for some restraint.

In an effort to contain the aggressive spread of another one-time favorite of the SCS, the autumn olive (*Eleagnus umbellata,* "olive-chaste tree with umbels"), native to eastern Asia, restrictions have lately been placed on its planting. Wayne tells me something of its history with the SCS: "In the borrow areas of a dam—where you dig up dirt to build the dam—down in the clay and soil where plants don't grow well, we'd set out autumn olive. Wonderful wildlife food, berries about as big as a pencil eraser—a friend in the Soil Conservation Service made jelly out of them." Then he outlines the problem: wherever autumn olive is set in, it asserts its thickety dominion and elbows out all other greenery, from grasses to trees. Limits have since been put on its use, and its sale west of the Blue Ridge in Virginia is now prohibited. (But commercial mail-order nurseries advertise its appeal both to wildlife and to jelly makers, and you can order it, no questions asked.)

Their talk reminds me of other Pinocchio plants that were brought to the U.S. with entirely benign intent but, once estab-

lished, quickly naturalized themselves, spread out, and created problems. Melaleuca (*Melaleuca quinquenervia*, "black-and-white tree with
five-ribbed leaves"), native to Australia and sometimes called bottle-
brush or honey myrtle, proceeded to help itself to large chunks of
southern Florida's wetlands, including the Everglades, after its introduction in 1906. And where it takes hold, it crowds out native vegetation and wildlife and offers them no possible means of return. Fortunately, the rest of the United States is exempted from invasion by
melaleuca's aversion to frost. Many parts of the Southwest, however,
have been overrun by a Eurasian tree sometimes called the "kudzu of
the West." It's the salt-cedar (*Tamarix chinensis*, "Chinese tamarisk"),
named for its salt-retaining leaves, which was introduced in the late
1700s and planted along streams as a resource for pioneers seeking
wood and flood control. It showed nothing but modesty during its
first century here, but then it reached out and now occupies more
than a million acres, no end in sight. Sopping up water from the
rivers and dammed impoundments of a basically dry and thirsty
land, it sends the vapor into the air, and when the leaves are shed,
the salt they contain poisons the soil against other kinds of growth.

And these are only a few of the pest plants now on the ram-
page. In the matter of kudzu, Bobby again begs me to be kind. But
there's no other choice. The SCS faced formidable challenges—a
country out of work, the South turned into a wasteland—and did
the best it could with the knowledge and means at hand. It's fair, I
think, to say that kudzu helped in no small way to save the South.
And it's angels like Wayne Hypes, like Bobby himself, who have
done the rest, setting out and carefully cultivating modern methods
of farming, soil restoration, and conservation.

In 1953, kudzu's bad manners—its utter lack of restraint, its reckless
tendency to barge in where it wasn't wanted—led the U.S. Department of Agriculture to delist it as one of the cover plants allowed
under the Agricultural Conservation Program. But only in 1962,
nine years later, did the SCS stop recommending its use in devel-

oped areas (a too little, too late response for which Bobby Whitescarver and Wayne Hypes can hardly be castigated). Finally, in 1970, the USDA gave it official status as a common weed in the southern U.S.

How sluggish, bureaucracy! How swift and all-encompassing, the newfound weed! Kudzu has virtues, yes, some of which have been put to good use during the century-plus of its tenure here: it is ornamental; it provides good fodder, though the yield per acre is low; and it holds poor, washed-out soil in place. Nowadays, in these three areas, technology and horticulture provide far better choices. Yet kudzu is here to stay. As we slide toward the millennium, little has changed—except that there's more of the stuff than ever before. Nor can we really hope to grub it out.

It may be that the vine has put a lock not only on the Southern landscape but also on American ways of seeing it, with bright, well-meaning people taking a dark and hostile view of an alien species. Certainly, on its own green terms, kudzu has achieved a spilling-over, almost enviable success. Perhaps we're put off, even frightened, by its sheer abundance, and the silent speed with which it grows.

> Japan invades, Far Eastern vines,
> Run from the clay banks they are
>
> Supposed to keep from eroding,
> Up telephone poles,
> Which rear, half out of leafage,
> As though they would shriek,
> Like things smothered by their own
> Green, mindless, unkillable ghosts.
> In Georgia, the legend says
> That you must close your windows
>
> At night to keep it out of the house. . . .

So begins "Kudzu," the eerie poem composed by James Dickey (1923–1997), a Georgian who knew most intimately whereof he spoke. There, the leeriness, the outright fear that it provokes, take the aspect of a recurrent nightmare that, like the eponymous plant, cannot be extirpated. In the poem, as in life, a man making his way through a tangle of kudzu may plunge unaware into a pit concealed by the leaves, and the venomous snakes that shelter unseen beneath the dense cover will strike both man and the cattle that are grazing there; the hogs, sent into the kudzu afterward, catch and fling upward, killing the "living vine" of each snake that they root out. Nor is there an end to terror. Even with the windows shut tight at night, there is no keeping out this immane green power. The one mortal recourse against the threat is to take on the nature of kudzu, to let its blind energy surge through the veins till a man becomes just as strong as the vine itself, and just as concealing, as friendly to serpents. Only then might his life receive the awe accorded to the vine—that it "prospered, till rooted out." Almost wistfully, I think, the poem seeks to soothe a pervasive human uneasiness in the presence of any thrusting, seizing, unstoppable force.

But the insinuation of kudzu into Dickey's lines and its possession of his poem is not the victory for *P. montana* that it might seem. The poet does not take on the nature of the vine; instead, he has seized it and bent it to a purpose of his own devising. Along with ornament, forage, and erosion control, another good use for kudzu: to provide the controlling image for a poem—the soil, so to speak, in which the words and music put down their roots. Nor, by more than a millennium, was Dickey the first to put kudzu to this kind of work; it fills the same role in the *Manyoshu*, a collection of Japanese poems which was assembled around A.D. 600.

So the result of kudzu infestation is not necessarily rage, despair, or bad language. And many people have discovered virtue where popular perception, especially in the American South, has all too often seen only vice. To begin with, *P. montana* can satisfy the three most basic human needs, those for food, clothing, and shelter.

From soup and salad to noodles and dessert made from its starch, kudzu has immemorially satisfied appetites in the Far East.

Certainly the Chinese popped kudzu into their mouths long before the vine was introduced into Japan sometime in the earliest centuries A.D. (The Chinese character meaning *kudzu* was imported along with the plant and has been used ever since by the Japanese.) The oldest surviving Japanese record of kudzu as a food comes from the 800s and notes that the leaves of wild vines were gathered and eaten as a vegetable. And it is thought that by the 1200s, the roots were dug so that their starch could be extracted both for everyday cooking and for the preparation of medicines. Little-changed over the centuries, the process of starch extraction—digging the roots by hand, cleaning, cutting, and pulverizing them, washing them over and again, removing impurities, forming the resultant paste into blocks and slowly drying it—is a labor-intensive, time-consuming enterprise that may take as long as ninety days. For Japanese palates, at least, the work is worthwhile. Stirred into sauces, soups, and even lemonade, the starch acts as a thickener every bit as effective as arrowroot and cornstarch, and maybe more so. It gives a crisp, delicate coating to foods rolled in it before they are deep-fried. As a jelling agent—and one sure to please a hard-core vegetarian—it ranks up at the top with gelatin. The leaves of kudzu may be steamed, eaten raw, or dried for crumbling into dough. Bees make a delicious honey from the fragrant purple flowers, and the flowers themselves may be pickled in vinegar or steeped for tea, from which jelly may be made. Actively farmed in Japan, kudzu vines are set into land that might not otherwise be put to human use, like the steep cuts along roads and railways, where they not only hold the soil but also provide a green view for the traveler's eye. But though it's a staple in Japanese kitchens, it's seldom found as a food in the United States—unless, of course, one encounters it by rumor, or comes across it in a health-food store, or wanders into Atlanta's Kudzu Cafe, which features a kudzu quiche among the exotica on its menu.

And what does kudzu powder taste like? No one in the boondocks of coastal North Carolina carries it, nor can I find a supplier anywhere near the small Virginia town in which we spend our winters. But I find an 800 number appended to an article on kudzu cookery in the *Atlanta Journal-Constitution*. The starch is in stock—hurray!—at a natural-foods wholesaler in Eaton Rapids, Michigan, just south of Lansing. The French-Canadian clerk (I asked her what accent I was hearing) wants to know how I'll use it—dietary supplement or what? For cooking, I say. Less than a week later, two pounds of Japanese-made kudzu starch arrive in the mail. The bag is filled with small, flat-sided chunks of a substance that looks like bone-white chalk. No eagerness touches my palate. Nonetheless, expecting to bite into something crunchy-chewy, I do pop a tiny piece into my mouth: no taste at all, it melts instantly and slides on down with silken ease. Seeing that I neither wince nor sputter, my husband, the Chief, pops one into his mouth, too. He nods. I have his assent, then, to use the starch not just in my food but also in dishes that are cooked for him. Stirring it beforehand into a little water, I add it to canned tomato soup and homemade gravy, both of which gain pleasant body. Unlike cornstarch or flour, it does not lump. Ideal stuff, I think, for thickening a gumbo. As for quiche, oh, yes: the Atlanta paper also printed the recipe from the Kudzu Cafe.

Whereas roots, leaves, and flowers all provide food, the ropey vines may be coaxed into yielding fiber. The traditional work of turning kudzu into filaments ready for weaving commands a week of scrupulous attention. The vines must be gathered when they are still young and flexible. Then they are cooked, wound into coils, and soaked in cooling water for a full day. The next step is fermentation, which decomposes the outer skin and allows it to be slipped off, revealing the two layers of fiber that enclose a woody core. More soaking follows. At last the cores can be extracted, and the fibers freed. They are made into loose hanks from which single strands of kudzu fiber are carefully pulled. The short strands are then knotted by hand into filaments, as long as 250 feet, that can be woven on a loom. The fabrics produced range from light ones with a tight weave and the shine of silk to loosely woven netting used to catch fish. Every step in the process, including the weaving, is done by hand. And the "grass" in the popular grass-cloth wallpaper is none other than kudzu, woven for the most part in South Korea, which, spotting a commercial winner, imported the vine from Japan. The fibers are also used to make decorative papers.

As for shelter, that use of the vine may not be an Oriental phenomenon. It may, indeed be restricted to the United States. But given the dense tangles formed by kudzu everywhere it grows, it's easy to imagine the inviting recesses, the cool and shadowy grottoes beneath the green leaves. I have, however, come across only a single record, which places kudzu housing right where it might be expected—in Georgia. The story, in the September 4, 1991, issue of the *Atlanta Journal-Constitution*, told of the threat that the planned construction of a new leg of the Presidential Parkway posed to the dozen or so homeless people who had taken up residence in the kudzu overrunning a vacant lot at Carter Center in Atlanta. I do not know their fate. But parkway or no parkway, it's nonetheless sure that city ordinances and social services (not to mention common decency) would not permit human beings to keep on living in quarters with high snake appeal but no plumbing.

The modern uses of kudzu don't stop with providing for the three basic human needs. The plant plays a not insignificant role in the traditional pharmacopoeia of Japan, China, Tibet, and many other countries of the Far East. There, herbal teas, brewed from dried roots sometimes mixed with other roots, seeds, and spices like ginger and cinnamon, have ever been imbibed to remedy a grand hodgepodge of ailments, including headaches, muscle stiffness, congested lungs and sinuses, measles, hangovers, and constipation. The white starch extracted from the roots may be eaten dry (take one chunk, let dissolve on tongue) or mixed with liquids to make a cream. The starch is considered every bit as potent as the teas against a host of discomforts and diseases, from obesity and a flaccid libido to gonorrhea, dysentery, and anemia. These days, cubes of dried root, along with starch for culinary or medicinal purposes, are available here and there in the United States at Oriental markets and stores devoted to natural foods or alternative healing methods. Some of these stores carry ready-made tea mixes and kudzu creams. Many do not offer the raw starch but sell instead nutritional supplements in the form of five-hundred milligram gelcaps, which contain the powder, often in combination with other herbs like Saint-John's-wort.

Kudzu might seem, at a superficial glance, to be a miraculous, all-healing remedy stirred up in the same kettle as the patent medicine of any snake-oil salesman. Recent research shows, however, that it may yet gain an honorable place in Western medicine. In 1992, the University of North Carolina at Chapel Hill issued a press release: David Overstreet and Amir Rezvani, both professors of psychiatry at the university's center for alcohol studies, had investigated an ancient Chinese application of a medicinal tea brewed from seven herbs, including kudzu. There, the tea has traditionally been prescribed not only as a relief from hangovers but also as a preventative for the overindulgence that causes hangovers in the first place. What real effects, if any, does the tea have on alcohol consumption? Working with David Lee, an organic chemist, Drs. Overstreet and Rezvani conducted experiments with three kinds of rats—Finnish, P-rat, and fawn-hooded—specially bred to prefer alcohol to water (like some people, some rodents not only relish booze but develop an addiction to it). Five of the seven herbs proved ineffective, but kudzu, refined to a chemical named puerarin by the researchers, served to reduce the impact of alcohol on the drinker and also to diminish intake. Similar work with a kudzu tea was announced in 1993 by Wing-Ming Keung and Bert L. Vallee of Harvard Medical School. Conducting their experiments with hamsters, the scientists discovered that animals injected with an extract from kudzu root reduced their alcohol intake by half, as opposed to the furry inebriates that had been injected with a substance containing no kudzu. These studies found that not one but two chemical compounds, which the researchers called daidzin and daidzein, were at work to reduce the desire to drink, as well as to make heads less tender and bellies less queasy the next day. It's a long way, yes, from rodents to *Homo sapiens*, but these experiments strongly reinforce the conclusions of Chinese folk practice.

And still no end to the uses of kudzu. Wherever it grows, its tough but flexible vines have furnished material for all manner of objects: tumplines, backpacks, and ropes for suspension bridges in Mongolia; birdhouses and rustic frames for pictures and mirrors in the American South, along with twisted wreaths, like those made of grapevines, for decorating front doors; and everywhere, baskets— dainty baskets the size of a small bird's nest, baskets big enough for a grown woman to sit in (if she so desires), and free-form and traditional baskets of every size between.

Then there's "Kudzu," the cartoon strip devised by Doug Marlette and now syndicated throughout the country. One of its main characters is the slightly befuddled Kudzu Dubose, an adolescent good old boy with high aspirations and acne-plagued skin. Another is the preacher, dressed circuit-rider style, who finds more trouble in technology than in the Devil. His church, of course, fields a youthful basketball team notable for falls and fumbles. Just as the plant has become the quintessential Southern vine, its cartoon namesake is a quintessential Southern way of pointing a finger at oneself and poking fun.

The almighty vine has also assumed an ineradicable position in the English language—that of an all-purpose pejorative epithet. Its application to salt-cedar—the kudzu of the West—has already been noted. The aquatic weed hydrilla (*Hydrilla verticillata*, "whorled waterplant"), another import from Asia, has been damned as "water kudzu" for the stealth and speed with which it covers ponds and dislodges native vegetation. Nor is condemnatory application of the word confined to the plant kingdom; like the vine, it shoots out and grabs whatever it can. An introduced Asian eel has been called "animal kudzu." The separatist members of a Georgia militia have been dubbed the "kudzu commandos."

And still no end to kudzu's deployment in the New World: although it's no longer the plant of choice for stabilizing soil and healing erosion, it is used to this day on precipitous embankments, and it continues to fill its two other early roles, those of forage and ornament. An American couple in the western part of North Carolina have devoted ten acres of their three-hundred-acre farm to the intentional cultivation of *P. montana;* after harvest, they either ensile or bale the leaves to serve as fodder for cattle and horses. And farmers in Alabama harvest wild kudzu for hay. In dry spells, especially, when other plants fare poorly, kudzu makes a crop because its root is able to tap deeply into sources of moisture. On a far grander scale, in 1990, the Japanese food-processing company Sakae Bio acquired 165 acres in Lee County, Alabama, strictly for the purpose of growing kudzu. Providing forage is not Sakae Bio's aim, however; this geographic outsourcing is meant to satisfy the human demands at home, where some fifteen hundred tons of the starch are consumed every year. In the realm of ornament, kudzu is still sold commercially to back-yard gardeners; my daughter-in-law Debra, who grows prairie plants in her small suburban yard in central Illinois (and also advises me on matters such as starlings), has found the vine in a local garden center, where it was labeled as an annual. Untrue, I thought—until Debra reminded me that killing temperatures of 25 degrees below zero are not uncommon in the great flatlands of the Midwest.

And who knows where the vine will pop up next?

Bane or blessing? Clearly *P. montana* is some of both, though the harm it does may well outweigh the benefits. Where the plant runs wild, it may destroy domestic species, especially young hardwoods, and it creates a self-sustaining monoculture that shuts out biodiversity not only in the vegetation but also in every other form of wildlife. But I'd like to quantify the economic damage wrought by kudzu, to learn its real costs to farming, forestry, and the taxpayer (to say nothing of the costs to utility companies and the budgets for railway maintenance). So I write to two government agencies, the department of agriculture and the department of transportation, in each of six Southern states: Georgia, Alabama, and Mississippi, the three that are most seriously overrun, plus North Carolina, South Carolina, and Tennessee. With the exception of Tennessee, which delivers only silence, the responses take one of two forms, depending on which agency replies. Agriculture, represented by the cooperative extension agencies, says, *Hmmm, interesting plant,* and sends informative pamphlets. The DOTs, responsible for keeping kudzu off the roads, speak with one voice: *Kill.* No one, however, provides any numbers. (Ironically, a USDA Forest Service publication, provided by the Mississippi Department of Agriculture and Commerce, plainly states that "lawmakers and public officials must be educated about the costs of noxious weeds" but gives no figures.)

I do gain other information. The plant is not troublesome enough in North Carolina for the state to declare it a weed. But few portions of this country are entirely safe from the deep roots and all-embracing vines; not even the Midwest with its arctic winters is free of the threat. While kudzu is happiest in the South's steamy heat, it will flourish almost anywhere, from the Atlantic to the Pacific, from the Canadian border to Mexico. The plant is capable of playing 'possum; the beholder is deceived by the fact that top growth is killed back by a hard frost. Beware: the root lurks underground unseen but quite alive. Once snuggled in, it becomes well-nigh unstoppable, absorbing nutrients from the soil and sending new leaves forth every spring to soak up necessary sustenance from the sun.

I learn, too, that for all its remarkable toughness, the plant is not immortal. It can be done in. South Carolina's DOT and its counterpart in Mississippi send lists of the herbicides that may be employed in the quest for annihilation. The names sound like a roll call of the Greek commanders who led their troops against Troy: amitrole, chlorsulfuron, clopyralid, dicamba, glyphosate, imazapyr, metasulfuron methyl, sulfometuron methyl, and paraquat. Some are selective, acting only on specific species; others kill every shrub, tree, vine, and blade of grass in sight. But herbicides alone won't conquer kudzu. There's one other ingredient without which nothing will be accomplished: persistence. The first few years of poison only discourage the vine; a full decade is required to do it in, a decade in which each sprout, each root crown must be relentlessly sought out and expensively sprayed. Even then, simply by sneaking under a neighboring fence or leaping from tree to tree, the villain may return, ready as ever to seize control. A spokesman for the Mississippi DOT says that herbicides merely keep kudzu at bay. (I've seen Mississippi kudzu along Interstate 55: for more than three hundred miles, from the Tennessee line straight on through Louisiana to the Gulf Coast, it swamps flat stretches of right-of-way with its huge green surge; its leaves, upholstering fences and brushpiles, turn them into overstuffed furniture for giants; its climbing vines convert trees and electric poles into long-necked and blowsy green dinosaurs.) And he offers the opinion that the only way to eliminate its dominion over the rights-of-way is to form anti-kudzu partnerships with adjacent landowners—together we stand, divided we give the vine permission to overrun and pull us down. His letter concludes with a wistful request that I let him know forthwith if I should come across any surefire methods for control.

(A goat, get a goat. Get any grazing or browsing animal. If the young shoots and leaves are regularly nibbled away and given no chance to regenerate, the roots will starve. But imagine Mississippi's highways, imagine any kudzu-threatened road, with goats, cows, horses, and sheep thronging the rights-of-way. Imagine the wrecked cars, the wrecked animals and people.)

Other methods of control include regular burning and cutting the foliage by hand. Several agencies are also trying to zero in on biological controls. Researchers at North Carolina State University have identified a native caterpillar, the soybean looper, as a creature with a usefully large appetite for kudzu; the trick, however, lies in connecting the caterpillars with kudzu leaves, which do not seem to lure egg-laying moths. Looking farther afield, the Forest Service studies the pathogens that infect the plant and the insects that feed upon it in China and Korea. To prevent new ecological disasters, perhaps greater in scale than that of kudzu, the biocontrols would not be transported here. Instead, a grand array of vegetation native to the American South would be taken to the Far East to see which, if any, species might be adversely affected. (Is it possible that one of these plants might be an American version of kudzu, a Pinocchio that runs away and grabs great chunks of the Orient?)

But kudzu can't be eradicated. Seven million acres and on a roll, it won't go away no matter what we do. Fire, chemicals, native predators, the backyard goat—all these amount to nothing more than temporary staying actions. What to do? Donald Ball, a professor and agronomist at Auburn University, sends me *Kudzu in Alabama: History, Uses, and Control,* an attractive pamphlet that he has cowritten with that state's cooperative extension service. In an accompanying letter, he writes: "Actually, I view kudzu not so much as being a despicable species as a multi-faceted species. . . . Furthermore, though not a native species, kudzu is so well adapted and widely established in the southern region that it has come to be associated with it and thus is part of our southern heritage."

Heritage, yes. And for all kudzu's tangible and widespread presence, its jack-in-the-box ability to pop up anywhere, he has also pointed out the invisible problem: How do we see it? American approaches typically range from disparagement to outright war—a war that the vine is preordained to win. Only an eccentric few of us find kudzu beautiful or worthy. And our perceptions both for and against depend, for the most part, on this criterion: Are we putting the plant to our own uses, or is it blindly, meanly appropriating something that we consider ours? In other words, who—or what—is in control?

Good, bad, or indifferent: no matter how we see it, kudzu has settled in and won't be budged. Roots in the earth, leaves to the sun, it will persist until the last trump. I've thought of comparing it to phenomena I find obnoxious, like the wild proliferation of pounding boom boxes or the unchecked spread of concrete lawn geese and decorative nylon banners, but no, there's nothing faddish about the plant. It's a force of nature, more on the order of azaleas and tobacco, country music, coon hunts, NASCAR races, and good old boys. It just plain *is*. Certainly, nothing obliges us to like it, but because we must live with it, the least painful way to come to terms with the doggone stuff may indeed be to see it as a heritage.

THE WISDOM OF NATURE

Brown-Headed Cowbird (*Molothrus ater*)

Brown-Headed Cowbird

I N early spring, I often hear the songs before I see the birds, little songs that tinkle lightly on the air like glass wind chimes. Then I'll spot a dozen of them, perched on a leafless mimosa or a black gum tree. The females wear a modest grayish brown, while the males are feathered in a glossy, iridescent black except for their heads, which are hooded in a rich golden-brown that is, not inappropriately, the color of a fresh cowpie. For these are brown-headed cowbirds, which hunt for their dinners in the vicinity of grazing cattle. Of all North American songbirds, the cowbirds alone are given to a most curious shiftlessness in matters of reproduction: dump and run, leaving not only their eggs but all parental responsibility to the harried care of a species other than their own. The brown-headed cowbird is known to parasitize at least 216 other kinds of birds, with the tally still mounting. And these days, this bird that puts the future of its species into a stranger's nest is found everywhere, from east to west, from north to south, clear across the country.

Once upon a time, not all that long ago, it was considerably more localized. In the days before Europeans discovered the North American continent and began barging across it, the brown-headed cowbird was found primarily in the central plains, with a range that more or less matched that of the plains bison. The bird followed the hooves of grazing bison or sometimes stationed itself right by an animal's head to batten on the insects stirred up as the great beasts moved and fed. Because of the close association, early observers sometimes called it the buffalo bird. Another fitting common name was cowpen bird, as in this description by Mark Catesby, the eighteenth-century British naturalist who wandered the colonies widely to collect botanical specimens and draw the birds, plants, insects, and animals of the New World:

> The bird is entirely brown, the back being darkest, and the breast and belly the lightest part of it. In winter they associate with the red-winged Starling and purple Jackdaw in flights. They delight much to feed in the pens of cattle, which has

given them their name. Not having seen any of them in summer, I believe they are birds of passage. They inhabit Virginia
and Carolina.

This description holds as true today as it did in the 1700s, except
that most observers—with one notable exception—have characterized the body of the male as black. Catesby's cowpen bird is often
seen abundantly amid the swarming winter flocks of the birds that
he called the starling and the jackdaw, birds known today, respectively, as the red-winged blackbird and the common grackle. It still
delights much to feed in the pens and pastures of cattle and horses.
And it is indeed a bird of passage, a migratory bird, although only
partially; its populations do not necessarily fly far from the breeding
grounds. Birds that summered and bred in northern parts may flock
slightly south for the winter, replacing birds that have themselves
flown farther south. The cowbird is also subject to what might be
considered a sudden whim—joining a fly-through flock of other
blackbirds. The species is certainly seen in Virginia and Carolina at
any time of year.

   The oddball observer was John James Audubon, who received
a pair of dead brown-headed cowbirds in 1824 from a friend and
proceeded forthwith to paint them. He called the species by two
common names, cow-bird and cow bunting, the latter because of
the stout, nearly conical bills, constructed like those of the true
buntings, grosbeaks, and finches. In both the initial watercolor and
the subsequent plate, Audubon's female cowbird closely resembles
the real thing; it is the male that astonishes. His head is shown in
the proper brown, and his body the proper black—except for the
wing, which displays a vivid swash of Delft blue that extends into
the tail feathers. Was the male bird sent to him somehow damaged?
Had artistic license overtaken the sensory evidence? We'll never
know. But we do know that Audubon was boggled by the bird's
dump-and-run proclivities. "If we are fond of admiring the wisdom
of Nature," he wrote, "we ought to mingle reason with admiration."
Then he noted the bird's unadmirable habit of laying its eggs in the

nests of other species to the great disadvantage of the "foster parents" and their eggs, which contained chicks doomed to perish. But, bowing somewhat grudgingly to powers greater than himself, he remarked, "This is a mystery to me; nevertheless, my belief in the wisdom of Nature is not staggered by it."

Cowpen bird, cow bunting, brown-headed cowbird—whatever its common name, it is formally known as *Molothrus ater*, the "black parasite." It is a member of the Icteridae, the New World's indigenous, well-populated blackbird family, which includes not just the often showy blackbirds (like the red-wings with red and yellow epaulets, the yellow-heads with golden helmets) but also the meadowlarks, the flashy orioles of North and South America, the grackles clad in shimmering black, and two groups found only south of the border: the sturdy caciques and the colonial oropendolas, both of which weave basket nests. Nor is the black parasite alone in its genus but shares it with four others. Only one of those four is also found in the continental U.S., most often in the southern part of Texas and occasionally in southernmost California and New Mexico—the bronzed cowbird (also known as the red-eyed cowbird), *M. aeneus*, the "brassy parasite." The remaining trio consists of Central and South American species: the bay-winged cowbird, *M. badius;* the shiny cowbird, *M. bonariensis;* and the screaming cowbird, *M. rufoaxillaris.* One other bird, of a different genus, also belongs to this gang for reasons of anatomy and behavior—the giant cowbird, *Scaphidura oryzivora,* which is also of the dump-and-run persuasion. Its formal name means something like "hard-digging rice eater," but the word *Scaphidura,* which may refer to the bird's conical, finchlike bill, is hybrid Greco-Latin invented by a taxonomist; it makes no good classical sense.

The single exception among the five *Molothrus* species to the parasitic mode of living is the South American bay-winged cowbird, which appropriates a nest built the previous season by another species and then actually tends the eggs that it lays there. Curiously enough, it is this species—exclusively this species—that is parasitized by the screaming cowbird, its close cousin. The giant cow-bird is almost as fussy, choosing primarily to parasitize members of its own blackbird family, the oropendolas and caciques. The other cowbirds are far more ecumenical, with 71 species recorded for the bronzed cowbird and 176 for the runner-up, the shiny cowbird. The brown-headed cowbird still leads the flock. The Plus-Minus style of symbiosis that cowbirds inflict on other species—and in their spe-cial, stealthy avian fashion—is known as brood parasitism. The females stow their offspring in another bird's brood by depositing their eggs one at a time in other birds' nests, usually after the nests are completely built and most often early in the morning when rightful proprietors are likely to be absent for a short stretch of time. When the egg is laid, the cowbirds fly away, shrugging off all fur-ther care. All that might be said in their favor is that the brown-headed, bay-winged, shiny, and screaming cowbirds are monoga-mous—no fooling around during the breeding season. But parasitism is without doubt a most peculiar way of life that leads me to ask why cowbirds behave as they do.

Gordon Orians, professor of zoology and environmental stud-ies at the University of Washington, has investigated the cowbirds' seeming lack of parental feeling and responsibility. After all, most other birds not only recognize their own nestlings, sometimes amid a host of look-alikes, but also tend assiduously to the successful fledging of their young. Only one percent of all birds are brood par-asites, most of them—mainly geese and ducks—intraspecifically amid their own kind and a few interspecifically with birds unlike themselves. Among the latter, the cowbird, along with the Eurasian cuckoo, is the prime example. With the exception of the moments of actual mating, it gives every single task of reproduction to others. And those others do all the hard work: build the nest, incubate the eggs, carry away eggshells after the hatch and fecal sacs after each feeding, and hunt from dawn till dusk to satisfy the bottomless appetites of insistent nestlings. Of those nestlings, the cowbird is usually the largest, able to seize every morsel of food brought in by the adult birds. To understand the cowbird's unbirdly behavior—how it came to abandon the usual parental role and how its habits affect both its own species and its hosts—Orians has asked five questions. How did brood parasitism start? Why did this habit spread? What changes, if any, has it caused in the behavior of parasite and host? How do changelings hatched in another bird's nest know what kind of bird they are? Is there communication between cowbirds and their hosts?

The answers to the first two questions must be speculative. No one was there to observe the aboriginal intrusion of a cowbird into the nest of a bird unlike itself or the subsequent behavior of that cowbird's duly hatched and fledged descendants. Though egg dumping—the occasional deposit of one bird's eggs in another's nest—is observed in many species, obligate brood parasitism is such a rare trait that its arrival on the avian scene is like a most peculiar and perverted accident. Its origin seems explicable, however, through looking at costs and benefits: at some point in the invisible reaches of the past, the hatch rate for the ancestral cowbird's dumped eggs and the fledging rate for her chicks must have been high enough so that it paid her and her offspring to continue taking advantage of the neighbors. As for the habit's spread, it may have to do with the fact that, with the single exception of one duck species, all brood parasites are altricial—born naked and blind, that is—and require several weeks of intensive feeding with high-protein food, mainly insects, before they can fledge. Though the adults are also granivorous, eating seeds, cowbirds have always relied to an almost perilous degree on the movements of large grazing animals—bison, horses, cows—to stir up the necessary insects as they move and munch. It is not always easy to find such conditions. "This suggests," Orians says, "that parasitizing the food-gathering abilities of host parents is more important than parasitizing their egg-covering abilities." Other inducements may have included fewer forays by predators on the hosts' nests than on the cowbirds', and an advantage in size—and thus in food-grabbing power—for cowbird hatchlings over their nest mates. Orians also posits a gradual beginning to brood parasitism, with eggs laid in foreign nests only now and then at first. But when successes began to outweigh failures, natural selection kicked in and set the cowbird on its future course.

How are the host birds to respond? The intruders' success often works to the hosts' detriment, drastically reducing the number of their young that fledge. Logic says that repeatedly parasitized species—red-eyed vireos, Eastern phoebes, lark sparrows, rare Kirtland's warblers, and the hundreds of others—would have evolved defenses over the millennia to protect their young. And indeed, a few have, but doing so must have been an almost fatally slow process. While birds recognize their own young, they rarely distinguish one egg from another. The basic syllogisms in a bird's brain may be stated this way: eggs in nest implies that the nest builder laid them; young bills agape stimulate the parent to invest in its own genetic line, the hatchlings in its nest, bringing them food and ignoring any other birds. Given these general rules of behavior, it's a matter of astonishment that any birds have been able to respond in a no-nonsense fashion to the cowbird threat. Yet a few species, like the gray catbird, the American robin, and Bullock's oriole, have become knowing rejectors, rather than unwitting acceptors. Experiments have shown that the female Bullock's oriole can indeed spot a foreign egg, and not just that of a cowbird but also of occasional egg dumpers like the loggerhead shrike and the house finch. She evidently learns to recognize her own eggs in a brief but crucial time that begins a few days before laying and ends when her first egg is placed in the nest. Just how she comes by this knowledge is still a mystery, but, as if she were picking up trash with a spike on the end of a long stick, she uses her bill to pierce the odd egg and cast it out. Some other songbirds also seem able to spot a ringer but are too small to use the oriole's tactic; they may either desert the nest and their own eggs or—as in the case of the yellow warbler, for one— reline the nest with a new floor that covers the old clutch, which will never hatch. There are no guarantees, however, that the rebuilt nest will not be parasitized. Yet the rejectors are few, and most species remain acceptors. Perhaps they've only recently been plagued by cowbirds, or, if the phenomenon of parasitism is not recent, circumstances were likely not conducive to the kinds of genetic change that would lead to the recognition and rejection of cowbird eggs.

How do young cowbirds know what they are? With many kinds of fowl, like geese, ducks, and chickens, imprinting is the secret: the first living creature the young bird sees gives it an identity. It will look to that creature for guidance in behavior and eventually seek a mate of that particular kind. This visual means of targeting a sense of self works perfectly when the creature seen is of the same species, but woe betide the gosling or chick led by first sight to think that it is something other than poultry, and in some cases that it is human. Other kinds of birds may also develop crippling attachments to humankind. My veterinarian daughter, who has worked to rehabilitate wild birds from various owls to a grown but featherless goldfinch, tells of an immature bald eagle returned to the greater world after months of mending in a cage: the bird had become so dependent on its keepers that after release, it would swoop down exuberantly and land on any handy human being just as if it were homing in on a parent. It could no longer fend for itself in the wild; recaptured, it will live out its days as a show-and-tell bird at a raptor rehab center. These birds with identity crises will fail at reproduction. But for cowbirds, despite the fact that the first creatures they see are birds totally unlike themselves, there seems to be no confusion, nor is there one jot of evidence that cowbirds have ever signally failed to perpetuate their kind. Researchers investigating the matter of how brown-headed cowbirds establish species identity have found that females raised in captivity respond with copulatory postures not to the songs of red-winged blackbirds, meadowlarks, or grackles but only to the lisping, tinkling wind-chime songs of males of their own kind. The knowledge of what they are is instinctive.

When it comes to communication between cowbirds and the species on which they batten, nothing could be more polite. The parasite will approach a potential host and offer something called a preening invitation display: stepping up close, bowing its head, and fluffing out its feathers. Often, the host will accept the invitation and proceed to groom the cowbird's feathers. And in a strange twist, some birds that do not engage in mutual preening among themselves will also respond in a positive fashion to the come-on of a cowbird. Observers think that such behavior may work both to calm aggressive tendencies in the host and to ease the way for the cowbird's entry in the carefully selected nest. The eggs, however, are laid when the host is absent.

And still no end to the questions. Orians also asks, Why did brood parasitism evolve in the cowbirds and in no other group of New World song birds? Why is there but a single species of cowbird over most of North America? And why, he wonders, do some kinds of cowbird parasitize many hosts, while others are limited to a few or, in the screaming cowbird's case, to only one? Here are puzzles not just for professional research but also for investigation by the educated amateur (if curiosity is not dampened altogether by despising the cowbird's habits).

One matter that is not a puzzle is the reason that the brown-headed cowbird has dramatically expanded its range in the last three centuries from the grassy, bison-friendly prairies to the country's entire sweep. The bird has simply followed our lead. We've facilitated an increase in its range and its numbers by clearing forests in favor of farms (more grain, more grazing livestock stirring up bugs) and also by establishing more forest-field edges (easier access to host nests) as we alter the landscape to develop living spaces for ourselves.

It may not be amiss to remember, too, that what cowbirds do is the birdly equivalent of leaving an infant on the doorstep of a church or a hospital: someone will accept the babe and care for it. The offspring's welfare is the prime consideration. The differences are two. First, the human mother practices parasitism on her own kind, while the brown-headed cowbird ventures forth and is parasitic only on species other than its own. Second, and more important, the human action is facultative, while that of the bird is obligate. In other words, the woman has options, but, in the wisdom of nature, the bird has been given no choice at all.

THE DEW LOVERS

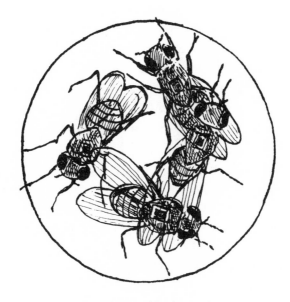

Fruit Fly (*Drosophila melanogaster*)

Drosophila Fruit Flies

THE sassy little fruit fly that is sometimes called a vinegar fly
evokes a full range of human responses in the people I know,
from outright loathing through amused tolerance to the
most ardent boosterism.

My husband, the Chief, for example, hates them. He does not
cotton to any common arachnid—spiders, ticks, and chiggers—nor
is he fond of mosquitoes, Japanese beetles, and tobacco hornworms,
but his attitude toward all of these is live and let live. The one form
of life that he most truly and passionately despises is fruit flies. They
insinuate themselves into our North Carolina mobile home through
doors opened in passing or the mesh of screens. They hover thickly
around the cantaloupes ripening on the kitchen counter and over
the bananas the Chief uses in his peanut butter sandwiches. They
cluster on the tomatoes he's brought inside to mature. They drown
in his diet cola and his beer. And, oh, they are canny at sneaking
into the freezer, where they become entombed in ice cubes. They
are even bold enough to investigate his person, winging silently in
front of his face, landing lightly on his T-shirt. He swats them, but
as soon as one is gone, another takes its place. I do not understand
this enmity. For fruit flies neither sting nor bite. They can be annoy-
ing, yes, but in a mild way, and when summer vanishes into fall,
they also vanish (though I've known them to resurface in winter
when we visit the trailer and turn on the heat.)

My daughter Elisabeth, the veterinarian, belongs, however, to
the tolerant camp. She lives year-round with fruit flies that are a naturally occurring by-product of something that I invariably think of
as The Habitat. Once upon a fairly recent time, when she and I
were driving down a narrow street on the outskirts of my small Virginia town, she spotted an Eastern box turtle moving like an eight-
inch tank along the side of the pavement. At her command, I
stopped and backed up. She scooped up the turtle, which sensibly
withdrew into its shell—a damaged shell with a great but well-
healed gash three inches long near the crest. As soon as she saw
that, the turtle received a name: Crash. Crash was then identified as

a male because of his red eyes and concave plastron. She took him to her Midwestern home—husband, children, cats, dogs, and sometimes wild birds, like great horned owls, that she is rehabilitating. There, amid the mob, Crash was installed in a large aquarium fitted out with a floor of wood chips, leaves, and other dry material. And there he lives today, though his surroundings have changed somewhat. Earthworms now inhabit the lower levels of the flooring; when Crash is struck by a craving for meat, he roots around for them. The thick layer of wood chips on the surface has turned into a fine, feathery stuff like dried grass, and in it three American toads have made burrows for themselves. The surface is also covered in one corner with Crash's preferred food, vegetables and fruit (as box turtles age, their tastes become more vegetarian). And over the potato peelings, old carrot tops, brown banana skins, chunks of melon, and other rotting comestibles, the fruit flies swarm. They in turn serve as snacks for Crash and feasts for toads. With The Habitat, a miniature ecosystem has been achieved. Luckily, the fruit flies stay confined within its glass walls, and so does the somewhat sour and fusty stench.

It's our friend Jay Hirsh, a molecular biologist and professor at the University of Virginia, who stands firmly with the boosters and studies the little fly with something akin to passion. He is among its premier proponents, the breeders and researchers who devotedly rear these creatures in the interests of science. Indeed, since the beginning of the twentieth century, scientists—geneticists, in particular—have swarmed around the little fly, attracted by its huge chromosomes and easily identifiable genes. These virtues have led to its use in highly successful studies: providing proof of Gregor Mendel's theory that physical characteristics are heritable, parent to offspring; developing gene-mapping techniques; and establishing that chromosomal changes lead to heritable variations. Only recently, Jay's small but dedicated group of researchers has conducted a series of experiments that expose the little flies to crack cocaine, about which more shall be set forth shortly. First, it must be said that messing around with fruit flies has more than once provided entry to a Nobel Prize. In 1933, Thomas Hunt Morgan received the Nobel Prize in Physiology or Medicine for work with fruit flies that revealed the chromosome theory of heredity—that the linkage of genes on chromosomes accounts for distinct hereditary traits. Thirteen years later, in 1946, Hermann Joseph Muller won the same prize for demonstrating that X-rays can speed the rate at which genetic mutations occur in these tiny, winged insects. In 1995, that prize was shared by three developmental geneticists, the American Edward B. Lewis, Christiane Nüsslein-Volhard of Germany, and her American colleague Eric F. Wieschaus, who used the little flies to discover the genetic controls for the early development of the embryo.

What are these flies anyhow? To begin with, they belong to the order Diptera, "two-wingers," which first received its name from the Greek philosopher and naturalist Aristotle. The Diptera are far and away the most despised creatures in America, and they comprise a vast, multifarious tribe that includes formidable members like houseflies and hard-biting horseflies, blowflies, botflies, and the tiny blackflies that make a misery of summer nights. And some kinds of fruit flies are surely as pestiferous as any of these, wreaking havoc on both human pocketbooks and peace of mind. Science has sorted the insects commonly called fruit flies into two families, the Tephritidae, or "ash-colored" family, named for the generally gray to black bodies of its members, and the more colorful Drosophilidae, or "dew-loving" family, named for its most common source of sustenance. The ash-colored flies, sometimes known also as the Trypetidae, or "borer" family, are generally much larger than the dew lovers, two- or three-tenths of an inch to the smaller flies' seven- or eight-hundredths, and it is this family's larvae that are able to bore into every part of a plant, from root and stem to leaves and fruit, and so bring devastation to field crops and orchards. In their number are pests like the apple maggot, which also dines on pears, plums, and blueberries. The Tephritidae also include a great gaggle of species

that feast selectively but voraciously on such economically important plants as celery, cherries, and olives. The black-bodied Mediterranean fruit fly—the Med fly notorious for ravaging citrus groves—
is one of them. Some of these ashy fruit flies, however, are known to
content themselves with goldenrod, while others breed harmlessly
in the heads of composite flowers like daisies. The Swiss zoologist
Walter Linsenmaier, known especially for his meticulously rendered
paintings and drawings of insects, has this to say about the Tephritidae, noisome or not: "The little fruit flies . . . are striking because of
their particularly beautiful wing designs." And the wings of many
family members are indeed lovely, patterned with delicate geome-
tries of light and shadow. But it's not the ashy flies that drive the
Chief to desperation and bad language, not these that feed my
daughter's turtle and toads or pave the way to Nobel Prizes. The
dew lovers, though they're little things to look at and clearly
unaware of their own importance, fill these roles.

The dew lovers by whatever common name they're known—
fruit flies, vinegar flies, pomace flies—ignore the crispness of an
apple on the tree or the melon still growing on the vine. Vinegar
and pomace: these names point to their fondness for spoiling fruit,
for the ooze of a decaying peach, the mush and ferment of a tomato
going bad. And this is the "dew" that these tiny flies love, this ooze
and mush. More particularly, it is the yeast of the fermentation
process on which they feed. They also lay their eggs in rotting fruits
or fungi, which provide an instant yeast supply for the newly
hatched larvae. These maggots are so small, matching the adult flies
in length, that they hardly seem in the same league as the much
larger larvae—the soft, pale, squirming get of house- and horseflies—usually thought of as maggots. In their penultimate stage, the
larvae pupate and then emerge as adults by way of a curious mecha-
nism called a ptilinum, a sac on the front of the head that alternately
swells and shrinks and works like a piston to break open the hardened pupal casing. On emerging, the heads of the new adults are
huge with fluid, and their wings are tiny, flat, and intricately folded.

Flight is achieved after the flies do something that Jay Hirsh calls "blowing up their wings": they use the muscles in their heads to pump the fluid rearward to expand and straighten the wings. The adults, females slightly bigger than males, are well equipped with both small hairs and bigger hairs called sensory bristles—on their heads and bodies, their legs, the edges of their wings, and also on the surface of the wings—though it takes a magnifying glass or microscope to see them well. On their forelegs the males have special hairs called "sex combs" that are used to stimulate female interest. But, unmagnified, the flies merely look a little fuzzy. There are about one thousand species of these flies, which are found the world around, and every one of them belongs to the genus *Drosophila*, the "dew lovers." Their colors, anatomical arrangements, and mutations are many: classic red eyes or aberrant white eyes; wings long, short, vestigial, or curly; bodies colored in earth tones—russet, dark gold, warm cider brown, with sooty rings around the plump abdomens of the males. These, with other features, occur in a gallimaufry of combinations. But no matter what they look like, their lives are uniformly short: twelve to fourteen days from egg through pupal stage and, under laboratory conditions, a few weeks to a month or two of adulthood. The brief life cycle may be timed to the here-today, gone-tomorrow nature of decaying fruit.

In part, it's the short life span that has made the dew lovers attractive to researchers in the last century. The little flies have been around long before humankind came down the pike—and they were surely on hand for Eve's famous chomp into the apple, a fruit as irresistible to a vinegar fly as it was to the woman, although for different reasons. Nor have they been neglected in the realm of poem. John Milton, for one, called on them to provide a simile in *Paradise Regained*. Satan, vanquished, tries to fend off the troubles caused by his "bad success," but they come back unceasingly ". . . as a swarm of flies in vintage time,/About the wine-press where sweet moust is power'd,/Beat off, returns as oft with humming sound." It might be argued here that Milton was referring to some other sort of fly, for fruit flies are not given to humming in a way perceptible by humankind, but Milton's venue is entirely correct—the must, which is the pressed-out juice and the pulp and skins of crushed fruit, along with the yeasty ferment of wine making.

Scientific use of the dew lovers started in earnest as the nineteenth century rolled into the twentieth. And one species in particular, out of the thousand species available, has become the star of research projects: *Drosophila melanogaster*, the "black-bellied dew lover," so named for the dark striping of the gaster, or abdomen, in the male. It was in 1909 that the future Nobelist Thomas Hunt Morgan chose *D. melanogaster* as an experimental organism, first for the mapping of chromosomes and then for investigations of genetic inheritance. Use of this particular species then spread from Morgan's "flyroom" at Columbia University because he and his colleagues frequently contributed not only their stock of knowledge but their stock of experimental flies to other laboratories. Because these little flies live only briefly but breed prodigiously, many generations can be produced during the course of any given study, and changes from one generation to the next can be followed quickly. Also, the flies have only four chromosomes, which are ribbonlike in the salivary glands and one hundred times the length and thickness of the average chromosome. Only an ordinary microscope needs to be used to map the genes of such giants as objects lined up and linked in a series. Thus, researchers have been able to determine exactly the inheritance of traits and, recently with Nüsslein-Volhard, Wieschaus, and Lewis, to find and identify 140 of the genes that are crucial to embryonic development.

Why be concerned about the embryonic development of a *fly*? And why subject a fly to crack cocaine? I visit our friend Jay in his lab at the University of Virginia. En route, I think to myself that mad scientists come in two varieties, those who create Frankensteins and those who play with fruit flies. Jay, trained as a biochemist but converted to molecular biology, is decidedly of the latter persuasion. He's a slender man, now in his early fifties, with a lean El Greco face and a short, neatly trimmed dark beard that is beginning to grizzle. And he's a man with talents that I find even more arcane than his cutting-edge research with fruit flies and cocaine. Jay can and does perform astonishing feats like fixing balky plumbing, mending broken appliances, and repairing cars. In his lab, he is the consummate scientist, introducing me enthusiastically to both his students and his wild-type Oregon-R flies, one of the two strains of *D. melanogaster* most widely used by investigators. The other strain is the Canton-S. Both were captured near the beginning of the twentieth century, in Oregon and Ohio respectively. The strains are similar in most physical respects, but because there are what Jay calls "significant behavioral differences in learning and memory," the strain used at the start of an experiment is always precisely specified.

"We study behaviors here that are very robust, *not* finicky," Jay says. And the flies are to be seen, safely bottled, in every nook and cranny of his lab, which came into being in January 1991, when he transformed a large area used for storage into a research facility. There is the high-bench area where experiments are performed on waist-high counters, from which rise tiers of shelves, like library stacks, that are filled with books, beakers, vials, microscopes, computers, and television monitors. The low-bench fly room, with counters at desk height, is decked out with similar equipment, plus dissecting microscopes and a swarm of clipped-out comic strips taped to the walls. Then, around the corner, is the nameless L-shaped room in which crack cocaine is administered to small, carefully monitored batches of flies. There, one of Jay's graduate students, Rozi Andretic, a lithe redhead from Croatia, also studies the genetics of the flies' circadian, or daily, rhythms of activity and quiescence (these are the rhythms that, when they are disrupted, cause jet lag in human beings); she particularly investigates some mutants that do not respond at all to alternations of light and darkness. "Wine flies," she calls them, translating *vinske mušice,* their name in her native language. This room also contains two walk-in closets filled floor to ceiling with vials of flies. One is used for quarantining new arrivals, dispatched by mail from various labs, including a fly bank at Indiana University; the newcomers need to be isolated lest they carry pests, like mites, that are inimical to the flies and, thus, to the experiments conducted here. The other closet is a dark, chilly place, kept at 18 degrees centigrade (64.4 degrees Fahrenheit) to slow down the development of stock not yet needed for any project. Though Jay calls these working quarters "low tech" because of the inexpensive components found throughout—the low-cost TV sets, for example, and the hair-dryer heating element that maintains a constant temperature for the flies during the experiments with cocaine—I find them to be an almost magical place in which tiny creatures are magnified not just into an easily observable size but into an amazing liveliness.

To introduce me to his tiny subjects, Jay first administers a knock-out dose of bubbling carbon dioxide to immobilize half a dozen black-bellied dew lovers. Peering at them through a micro-scope in the fly room, I see fruit flies as I've never seen them before—as whole creatures, not hithering, thithering specks of pro-tein. These are flies of the white-eyed sort; white, however, means only that their large eyes are not the standard fruit-fly red but rather the pale golden color of champagne. Their wings are elegant—panes of transparent crystal with fine black venation, like the clear leaded glass that one sees in churches and manor houses. Then I watch unsedated flies scamper, flit about, and groom themselves assiduously. Living as they do amid fermenting muck, they must keep their wings clean if they're not to become enmired in their food. Colleen McClung is also present in the fly room. She's another of Jay's graduate students and co-author with him of a recent paper on the lab's experiments with flies and cocaine. Young, blond, well tanned, wearing shorts, and sporting a toe ring along with toenails of iridescent frosted blue, she is busy putting instant fly food into a batch of clean bottles. It's green stuff, made of oat-meal and other grains and given its color by the addition of antibi-otic and antifungal ingredients, plus a dash of food coloring. The bottles, shaped like inverted funnels with a narrow neck and wide base, were originally manufactured for collecting urine samples, but they serve nicely indeed for housing fruit flies, with food at the bottom and flying space above. So that I can get a good, close look, the inhabitants of one bottle are magnified through a microscope, with their enlarged images projected onto a TV set. The adults flit busily about or groom themselves. I see one male lift a single wing and flutter it like a semaphore. He's doing something called "singing," or beating his wing so that it emits a low-frequency sound, inaudible to us but seductive to female flies. Meanwhile, the members of the up-and-coming generation—the larvae—have buried themselves head-first in the green glop that is their food, and their dark jaws work constantly, furiously, while their internal organs throb and their pale maggot bodies writhe with what seems a truly sensuous pleasure. The only stage of flykind not in motion is the pupal stage; the beige pupae, shaped something like tiny toboggans with squared-off ends, are attached to the bottle's walls.

And I learn from Colleen McClung that the scientists who play with fruit flies not only engage in robust experiments but do them with a sense of humor. They have a fine talent for coming up with memorably antic names for types of genes. Aside from fruit flies, one other creature is widely used for genetic research—the nematode *Caenorhabditis elegans*, or "elegant new-rod," for its rodlike shape—but the people who work with these worms assign them dour numbers rather than names. (It was announced in December 1998 that every last one of *C. elegans's* 19,099 genes have now been mapped—a considerable feat.) Colleen tells me with great glee that fruit flies, on the other hand, may harbor genetic mutations that are named after vegetables, like *rutabaga*, or after human counterparts, like *dunce* and *couch potato*. There's also *fruitless* for a gene dictating interest in the same sex, *tinman* for a gene that instructs its possessors not to develop a heart, and *groucho* for a gene causing extra bristles that look like bushy eyebrows to grow above each eye. And there's *ether-a-go-go* for a mutated gene that inspires shaking in the legs of anesthetized flies. For purposes of easy reference, all fly genes have been given two- or three-letter acronyms; for example, *ether-a-go-go* is known as *eag*.

Then I visit the nameless room, where crack is volatilized in a sealed glass chamber inhabited by flies. The puff of smoke is generated by low-tech means—cocaine put on a coil with a Radio Shack connector. The flies do not snort the crack—they're not built to inhale—but rather absorb it through cuticle and trachea. Their subsequent behavior is recorded and also projected, a hundred times larger than life, by a video camera with a macro lens onto a TV screen. These experiments are blind. To keep them as objective as possible, the researchers do not know how much, if any, crack has been applied to each coil until the tests are concluded and the results analyzed.

Why do this? To begin with, how did the idea of experiments using crack ever arise? *How* had to do, Jay says, with "an evolution of thoughts" and, particularly, with trying to understand a type of fruit fly that spent an abnormally great amount of time in grooming behavior. As for *why*, he says this: "Fruit flies are a lot of fun. The exciting aspect is that you can do real genetics with them. The early genetics of flies was basically stamp collecting and categorizing genetic lesions [changes] that affected the external morphology of the fly. It was only in the 1960–1970s that it was generally realized that mutations affecting behavior and development of the fly could be easily isolated, and in the last fifteen years came the realization that the genes involved in these processes are highly related to genes involved in similar functions in vertebrates."

His investigations began in a definitely robust way: decapitating the little flies so that there was direct access to the nerve cord. How do they stay alive without heads? Their nervous system kicks in and directs them to follow normal routines in such matters as standing upright and grooming. Headless, they can live for days if they're kept moist and don't fly away. The beheading technique was developed elsewhere several decades ago; at the outset it was a tool for investigating mate preference. Till recently, Jay used it, "like pouring drugs down a hole," to deliver various substances to his tiny subjects to see if they would stimulate grooming. Many of them did. He puts on a videotape of headless bodies variously, soundlessly slurping in droplets of cocaine and neurotransmitters like dopamine and octopamine. But experimenting with decapitated flies proved problematic: though grooming behavior may certainly be observed in headless flies, it is impossible to use them to study genetics. Males that lack heads won't mate; there are no progeny to track for genetic traits. Worse, without heads, there are no brains. The fly's brain, however, is a main concern for Jay and his colleagues, who are particularly interested in the region in which dopamine and related compounds act directly on the brain's receptors to control motor activities. Cocaine, on the other hand, does not itself act directly on the receptors but rather seems to work in flies, as it does in vertebrates, to prevent the uptake and clearance of dopamine and related compounds.

What to do? How to revitalize investigations that were not only headless but seemed at a dead end? And a solution had to be found within only a few months, for the project's grant renewal was coming up with the speed of a runaway truck. Jay says, "The key that broke all this open was that, at a meeting, I ran into a clinician who deals with cocaine addicts." The subject of crack cocaine came up—freebase cocaine that can be smoked, that can be volatilized. With the proper papers, crack is available from the National Institutes of Health. It was obtained. In January 1997 the experimental chamber was set up—crack going up in a puff of smoke. And the little flies, able to take in the smoke through their skins, now kept their heads. As it happens, fruit flies don't really like smoke, but as captives they have no choice.

As Jay worked on writing the new grant proposal, Colleen McClung designed and monitored the new experiments. She found that when cocaine in volatile form is given to fruit flies, it induces behaviors astonishingly similar to those of rodents subjected to the drug. Depending upon the exposure to crack, the little flies exhibit seven progressively more severe responses, which occur within the short time frame of only 30 to 150 seconds, while recovery takes five to ten minutes. Their normal behavior involves the activities that so irritate my husband—skittering, flitting about, and pausing every so often to groom themselves. The seven stages of intoxication as recorded by Colleen McClung are these:

1. Intense nearly continuous grooming and reduced locomotion.
2. Stereotyped locomotion, extended proboscis. Some locomotion with simultaneous grooming. In this stage and those subsequent, the subjects lose their ability to fly and remain at the bottom of the container.
3. Low stereotypic locomotion in a circular pattern, extended proboscis.
4. Rapid twirling, sideways or backward locomotion sometimes accompanied by a front leg twitch.
5. Hyperkinetic behaviors including bouts of rapid rotation, wing buzzing, erratic activity with flies often bouncing off the walls of the container.
6. Severe whole body tremor, no locomotion, usually overturned with legs contracted to body.
7. Akinesia or death.

In the nameless room, I watch a fly in the throes of stage 3: slowly, aimlessly, out of control, it circles and circles.

The most important discovery here seems to be that when intermittent doses of cocaine are administered, D. melanogaster develops a behavioral sensitization. "The most exciting part of our fruit-fly research is this weird process called sensitization," Jay says. A first exposure to low doses of cocaine has little effect on the flies, but subsequent doses give rise to what Jay calls a "locomotory stir." A sort of frenzied bustle kicks in; that is, the fly cleans or flicks its wings in an almost obsessive fashion. For reasons not yet known, male flies are affected more severely than females. The flies do not become addicted to the crack, but that is because, with no say in the matter, they either take what is given or go without. (The dew lovers are capable of making choices, but how choice might affect their approach to cocaine is a subject for future study.) To observe effects, however, is only to explore the surface of sensitization.

"The vertebrate genome," Jay tells me, "is basically a quadruplication of the fly genome with a bit of elaboration." And here is the greatest boon that minuscule D. melanogaster provides to the serious inquirer: though the fly is certainly small and spineless, it is nonetheless endowed with biochemical pathways remarkably similar to those of higher vertebrates, including rats and human beings. The phenomenon is one known as the evolutionary conservation of genetic pathways. When a biological arrangement works, there's no need for evolution to tamper with the basic model. Elaborate on, perhaps, but not redesign. And not only developmental but neural and behavioral genetics may be traced in fruit flies, along with those affecting learning and memory. Thus, if the genetic pathways of things like embryonic development, circadian rhythms, neural function, and sensitization to cocaine can be charted in fruit flies, then the findings may well be significant for us. One researcher with a special interest in courtship has written, "Human counterparts have already been discovered for a number of genes originally identified in the fly. . . . These findings should provide insights into the molecular interactions that enable the central nervous system to produce behavior." Thus, flies may tell us how a fertilized egg receives its orders to grow. They may also indicate how alcoholism, for example, and sensitization to narcotic substances occur in our kind.

The crucial part of Jay's experiments will be to chart the fundamental biological pathways involved in the flies' responses to cocaine. So far, given the evolutionary conservation of pathways, his research indicates that things happening within the microcosm of a fly—the stereotyped behavior, the hyperactivity, the tremors— can, and do, happen within a rodent, an ape, a human being. And if the mechanisms of response to cocaine can be understood, then it may be possible to find methods of preventing or blocking addiction.

Fortunately, there are enough dew lovers in this world so that the Chief in his swatting, spraying mode cannot conceivably cause any diminishment in the world's population. I doubt, though, that I'll convince him to stay his hand or lay down the can of repellent. Nonetheless, I'm on the side of the proponents. There's much to be said in favor of the little fly. It may be infinitesimal, but it holds infinite promise.

UNFINISHED BUSINESS

Snow geese (*Chen caerulescens*)

Homo sapiens

Man was nature's mistake—she neglected to finish him—and she has never ceased paying for her mistake.
        —Eric Hoffer, "On Nature and Human Nature"

WHICH species do you most despise? Which plant or animal do you think most pestiferous? Which would you like to see gone, and not just gone but gone forever? I solicit opinions from anyone who wants to answer. One Saturday afternoon, I posed the questions in Columbia, South Carolina, on the occasion of a lively book festival. I participated by telling a story from one of my books—telling because the six minutes allotted were enough for talk but not for reading the text except with unsuitably breathless haste. The final minute, however, was devoted to stating the questions about despicable species and requesting members of the audience to stop by afterward with answers.

And people did stop by to complain about and list their least favorite critters and weeds. Cockroaches led the pack with three votes. One vote each went to this hodgepodge of bugbears, harpies, and swatlings: pigeon, bat, mouse, opossum, squirrel, flea, gnat, mosquito, tick, chigger, cocklebur, and pines, not a particular species, like the loblolly, but all the durn pine trees in the world. One other animal may have received a vote, though it is hard to tell if the paragraph jotted on my notepad was meant to select a species or to deliver a short, emphatic lecture to the woman—me—who was asking silly questions. Signed "From a Zookeeper," it reads: "There are no despicable species—there is, however, ONE species which demonstrates great despicableness—the *only* species on earth that destroys the world in which it lives—the *human* species."

Zookeeper came, wrote quickly, and departed before I could note any details of age and gender. Conversation would have been welcome, along with Zookeeper's suggestions for ways in which our kind might learn to pick up the clothes, toys, fast-food wrappers, beer cans, and other detritus of our consumer culture that it strews in its own room.

But not everyone lives in middle-class comfort. Some of us live in mountain hollows or equatorial villages, on arctic islands or Asiatic steppes. Some people in this country live in cardboard boxes, on grates in urban sidewalks, or under the kudzu vines overrunning vacant lots. These rooms are strewn with hand-to-mouth necessity. The raw human search for food, fuel, and shelter leads to destruction. Birds lose the trees and grasses that they need for cover. Rivers run dry. The sands of the Sahel inch south a little farther every year. But who are we who live amid the comforts and luxuries—the delusive armor of technology—to tell those who lead hardscrabble lives that they ought to pick up their rooms and, while they're at it, limit their populations lest they starve? Control over reproductive life means individual freedom to some of us, but tyranny, mandated by the state or a privileged elite, to many others.

In 1711, Jonathan Swift's hero Captain Lemuel Gulliver was marooned on an uncharted shore by his mutinous crew. No stranger to fantastical adventure, he immediately set about seeking out the inhabitants of this land of pastures and tidy oat fields. He was sure that he could win the favor of any savages he might encounter, for he was well supplied with trinkets. The first living animals that he met were wild indeed—naked brown-buff creatures with no use for Gulliver's bracelets and glass rings. Though they bore a striking resemblance to humankind, they were endowed, male and female, with hairy chests and a ridge of fur down the center of their backs. Sometimes they stood on their hind legs, sometimes they went about on all fours, and all of them stank. Worse, when Gulliver took shelter under a tree, they climbed it most nimbly and shat upon his helpless head. "I never beheld in all my travels so disagreeable an animal," said Gulliver, "or one against which I naturally conceived so strong antipathy." He was rescued by two horses, one gray, the other bay, who turned out to be members of the land's dominant species, the Houyhnhnms. And these noble horses, dedicated to the use of reason in every aspect of their lives, kept the wild, stinking animals, which they called Yahoos, as beasts of burden and pullers of carts. The hides of the Yahoos were also turned into leather goods. Gulliver himself came to see the creatures as "the most unteachable of all animals, their capacities never reaching higher than to draw or carry burthens. Yet I am of opinion this defect ariseth chiefly from a perverse, restive disposition. For they are cunning, malicious, treacherous, and revengeful. They are strong and hardy, but of a cowardly spirit, and by consequence insolent, abject, and cruel."

From the beginning of his untoward adventure, Gulliver applied himself to learning the language of the Houyhnhnms and was soon able to converse at length with the horse he refers to as his master. Much of their talk consisted of questions and answers, with the horse earnestly interrogating Gulliver in an effort to understand his sudden apparition on these shores and to learn about his two-legged kind, and Gulliver responding at voluble and detailed length. As the years passed, one, two, three, Gulliver came so much to admire the horses' rule of reason that he wished to spend the rest of his days with these paragons of rational thinking and conduct. but after hearing descriptions of humankind as creatures who often sought their livelihoods by "begging, robbing, stealing, cheating, pimping, forswearing, flattering, suborning, forging, gaming, lying, fawning, hectoring, voting, star-gazing, poisoning, whoring, canting, libelling, free-thinking, and the like occupations," the Houyhnhnms declared Gulliver a Yahoo, albeit one with a semblance of reason, and bade him go. In the end, Gulliver himself came to think that "my family, my friends, my countrymen, or human race in general, when I considered them as they really were, Yahoos in shape and disposition, only a little more civilized, and qualified with the gift of speech." More terrible, the species of which Gulliver was a member employed their reason to multiply their vices and so exacerbate their degradation, while the Yahoos of Houyhnhnmland were only as barbaric as nature allowed.

Zookeeper would agree, I'm sure, that fiction echoes fact and that nothing has changed much in the last three hundred years.

How did we come to this not so pretty pass? An antic vision flits through my imagination:

There they are, the naked two of them, Adam and Eve, out there in that blasted thorn field. There's no going back to Eden, not with flaming swords barring the way. The two of them may be shivering. They're certainly wondering what happened. And here comes a snake, which seizes a frog and gulps it down whole. (Adam shudders.) Overhead flies a bird with grass for nest building in its bill. A cat tracks the flight with patient eyes, while its kittens play amid weeds and wildflowers. Over yonder, tiny flies swarm like motes of sunlit dust above the creek; a fish leaps open-mouthed. A mosquito lands on Adam's arm, another on Eve's right shoulder. Next thing they know, they're scratching and slapping and inventing the world's first invective. They also learn to pluck a leafy branch from the nearest tree, not to cover their pudenda—the parts, that is, they're supposed to be ashamed of—but to serve as a whisk and a surefire swatter. The problem is greater, however, than that of being preyed upon by a puny, six-legged insect with an unconscionably long proboscis. It's that they alone, out of all creation, don't quite know what they're doing. Everything else is perfectly at home, possessed of a niche and an inborn knowledge of how to live. But man and woman are restless, incomplete, unnatural, and probing always for something to ameliorate their psychic discomfort, which is as chronic and nagging as hay fever or a bad back.

The quest for remedies has come a long way—from the wheel to the Pentium chip, from cave paintings to computer imaging, projectile points to atomic weaponry, charms and healing spells to organ transplants, from the Ten Commandments and the Gospels to Einstein and to chaos theory. Man, according to Eric Hoffer

(1902–1983), the curmudgeonly longshoreman-philosopher whose aphoristic work was popular in the 1950s and 1960s, "has to finish himself by technology. . . . Lacking organic adaptations to a particular environment, he must adapt the environment to himself and re-create the world." And we, Adam and Eve's descendants, have truly, as Hoffer says, broken free from nature in many respects and removed ourselves from domination by her "iron laws."

But humankind once did occupy a niche. With an entirely appropriate metaphor, the ecologist Paul Colinvaux has defined "niche" as "more than just a physical place: it is a place in the grand scheme of things. The niche is an animal's (or a plant's) profession." Once upon a time, our profession was that of hunter-gatherers, seeking live animals for meat and collecting stay-put edibles like nuts and berries, insects, snails, and birds' eggs. It is part of today's conventional wisdom to ascribe to our tribal forebears a deep and healthy reverence for the natural world that provided them with meat and vegetables. I accept the existence of such reverence—it must have been as real as sun and rain, wind and the good earth— but I suspect that it sprang not from any phenomena outside the confines of the human body but rather arose out of that body's blind, unthinking, needy push to survive. Oak and bear and snake were worshiped not for their own sakes but in a cautionary way, for the benefits or harms that they could most certainly bring to our frail flesh. From seasons of plenty through seasons of dearth, the calories we earned were spent mainly on finding more calories. Our numbers were limited by the difficulties inherent in just getting by. It behooved us to revere the natural things whence came our strength, to appease the nonhuman powers arrayed against us, and to make our small magic lest we lose our lives.

For creatures such as we, capable of memory and forethought, the niche may have seemed as constrictive as outgrown clothes. But alterations were made some twelve to fourteen millennia ago when we discovered that animals could be tamed and plants made to grow in cultivated plots. Agriculture and animal husbandry have let us stay home, devoting less energy to the quest for brute survival and more to things like art, politics, and concocting remedies for everything, great or picayune, that bothers us. To this day, we struggle for completeness, if not perfection, and the effort has not been without success, at least in the realm of creature comforts. Although most of the planet's people still scratch out their livings in the thorn field, we who inhabit the industrialized West's neoparadise actively enjoy the apparent freedom from natural constraints that technology grants us. Nor are we mean enough to keep all the wealth to ourselves but parcel it out, sometimes efficiently, sometimes not. And all of us, those still caught amid thorns and those growing fat in a man-made Eden, increase our numbers, jostling and tripping one another as we crowd the earth. Human populations no longer depend on the cycles of nature for flourishing or failure. But these days, the only people who can afford reverence for earth, for plants and animals and stones and stars, may be those rich enough not to wonder where the next meal is coming from. We're still incomplete.

Yet how can better swatters and bigger mousetraps be enough to make us whole? How can computers and spacecraft and genetically engineered corn round off our rough corners, patch the cracks, and mend the recurrent breaks? Technology springs from human ideation. Then it's put together by human hands. A seized-up engine, however, is hardly the same as a myocardial infarction. Technology exists independently, not as part and parcel of our flesh and bones. It's armor, protecting the poor soft organism inside. Nor is it in any way finished. It can't be, not till we finish ourselves.

As the twentieth century wheels pell-mell into the twenty-first, the human situation is closely akin to that of the snow geese. What dramatically beautiful birds they are, entirely white except for their wingtips, which look as though dipped in midnight ink! I have seen the snows flying over the Neuse, their strong white bodies gathering up the last light and glowing against the gray of an evening sky. They fly far indeed, wintering on the mid-Atlantic seaboard, breeding in the Arctic tundra. But only a hundred years ago, at the turn of the last century, their wings were almost clipped forever; snow geese came within a feather of joining the dodo and the moa, the passenger pigeon and the Carolina parakeet in the dark realm of extinction. The cannonades of go-for-broke market hunting, along with wholesale slaughter on the nesting grounds, had diminished their number to a fragile few thousand. Thanks to protective legislation, however, and the creation of wildlife refuges, populations of snow geese have undergone an explosive recovery, with the species now totalling in the millions. Winter flocks more than half a million strong congregate these days in the salt marshes of the Delmarva peninsula. It might seem that they're out of danger, but no: they represent too much of a good thing. The problem stems from their not so dainty feeding habits. Not only do they relish the bird-attracting grains planted in refuges and nearby farms but they also instinctively grub out cordgrass (*Spartina alterniflora*), an important salt-marsh plant, then swallow its roots with great gusto, and go back instanter for more. In a phenomenon that wildlife managers call an "eatout," the living heart of the tidal marshes is devoured; where once acre on acre of tall cordgrass flourished, dry stalks rustling in the winter wind and roots waiting beneath the water for spring, mudflats remain. And the tundra of their breeding range—the Northwest Territories and Hudson Bay for the lesser snow geese, Baffin Island and even Greenland for the greater snows—is also being eaten alive. Nor can they be dissuaded from returning year-in, year-out to devastation. Waterfowl are often notoriously loyal to the same tiny patch of muskeg and moss where they themselves were hatched out, and they zero in on that one small spot to rear their own young. But more and monstrously more of them are crowding into the range with each passing year. In a book published in 1999, the naturalist and writer Scott Weidensaul, who has made an extensive popular study of migration, offers the inevitable comparison: "At last count there were more than half a million greater snow geese, and several million lesser snows—and both were continuing to increase at about 5 percent a year. Plot that on a chart and you get the sort of swooping, upward curve usually seen with articles on human overpopulation. And like humans, snow geese are consuming the very environment on which they depend."

What to do? Hunters' bag limits have been raised in some refuges, but the actual take of these birds has not made any dent at all in their gleaming hungry multitudes. Sooner rather than later, overpopulation will lead to starvation and disease. There is a gulf of difference, though, between the geese and us: the birds have no way to mend the ravages that they—and we in our zeal to protect them—have caused, but our kind holds its future in its own hands.

My friend Paul Cabe, the scientist who has provided me with much information about the swart and raucous lives of starlings, conducts genetic research these days on duckweed and also teaches environmental studies. He says, "Communities and ecosystems are not like engines—remove one part and nothing works, everything fails." And to their great aghastment, he tells his students, "For most species, extinction will not have catastrophic results. Other species will probably shift their abundance, but the world they live in will not disappear or fall apart."

To this it can be added that more often than not, extinctions are not noticed, not by ecosystem or community or ever-investigating, ever-nosy humankind. We are often not aware in the first place that a particular plant or animal, fungus, bacterium, or dinoflagellate had once had a lease on life but now is vanished from the earth. Nor has the absolute disappearance of these species impinged in any noticeable way—or in any way at all—on our two-legged, big-brained kind.

So what's the fuss about? Why work to save black-footed ferrets, torreya trees, and Wyoming toads, not to mention snail darters in Tennessee and California's minuscule Delhi Sands flower-loving fly? Are they necessary to the planet's spin? Ecological correctness shouts an immediate *Yes!* Reason takes a deep breath and says, *We don't know.* Reason also posits that they're highly localized species, all of them, and if they were gone, not just people but hardly any other living thing would miss them. Extinctions are a fact of natural life. Evolution, nonetheless, does not come to a screeching halt.

I think that one reason for the fuss—the often sentimental, sometimes woefully uninformed push to preserve, conserve, protect at all costs—has to do not with a sacredness supposedly intrinsic to all and any life but rather with a dimming of the rainbow's colors. And perhaps with the extreme endangerment of a peculiar, and peculiarly human—and hardly altruistic—sort of hope: if our behavior dooms species to sure vanishment, we may lose the magic plant or animal products that could cure us of mortality. There's something in the rage to preserve that speaks to an American fear of death.

The rage, however, is oddly selective. Nor do we have the courage of our common sense as often as we need it. If all humankind adhered to Jainism, an ancient and peaceful religion of India, everyone would follow the doctrine of *ahimsa* that prohibits doing violence to any living thing. Instead, we deem some lives worthy of defense but ignore, excoriate, or persecute others. Imagine a group calling itself People for the Ethical Treatment of Plants, and another called Save the Crustaceans. Trouble is, plants don't wag their tails or have big, love-me eyes; blue crabs and shrimp respond to us mainly by allowing themselves to be caught. If the life at hand is good to eat, it's fair game. If it annoys, stings, or sickens us, then we assume that we have leave to swat it, squash it, cut it down, or go all out to exterminate it.

Life on earth may well be compared to a rainbow. Red coexists here with purple and puce, along with the blooming or saddened rest of the spectrum. Blooming and saddening—the terms come from the dyer's trade and mean, respectively, brightened or dulled. In the best of all worlds there's room for both, as well as every tint and hue between. The scientists' term for the rainbow's colors is *biodiversity*. A ponderous catchword, but it means simply "variety of life-forms." Loss of diversity means proliferating shades of gray—more starlings, more kudzu, more molds, although (who knows?) evolution, irrepressible as always, might ring some startling changes on these all too familiar themes.

But variety of life-forms has nothing to do with quantity. Only theology asks how many angels can dance on the head of a pin. With biodiversity, it's quality and coexistence that count. Do cherubim and seraphim, powers and dominions leap and spin along with the angels? In more mundane terms, what array of life-forms—what wings, roots, and fins, what creeping, dividing cells—exists in a given place? Are the niches filled? Who comes to visit or stay? Who leaves never to return? And, with the bustling arrivals and departures, what changes for better or worse are wrought in the community?

Why be concerned in the first place? Because, I am sure of it, the human psyche needs a sense of wonder as much as the body needs food, sleep, and breath. Because living with shades of gray, with concrete, steel, and oil, casts a grayness into heart and mind. But with our burgeoning numbers, grayness is all but assured. The natural philosopher and ecologist Paul Shepard has put it plainly: "Large human populations tend to degrade the environment, both as a source of food and as a medium of biological richness. Complex brains are an adaptation to biological richness and therefore require interesting surroundings." Then, speaking of our multifariousness, he has said, "Environmental requirements are greater and more exacting for humans than for most other species. . . . A wide flexibility of behavior requires suitable environmental diversity." And humankind, so studies of environmental planning say, also requires several features in its surroundings in order to find the greatest ease: natural light (no windowless factories), greenery (the African savanna where man was born, our present-day lawns), water (ocean, creek, deep well, or artificial pond), and mysteries (unexpected turns in the path that reveal new vistas). These mysteries have been defined by one set of researchers as surroundings that "give the impression that one could acquire new information if one were to travel deeper into the scene." The mysteries have to do with expectations then, and with the promises that every environment, urban or rural, should make to those who live and travel there.

We cannot always predict how and when the promises will be fulfilled, but living amid a rainbow of other lives ensures the keeping of promises—a flower around this corner, a snake around the next.

We've made things hard for ourselves. Animalcules and tiny plants exist in uncountable trillions, but most large, predatory animals are scarce on the ground, for their numbers are set by the calories available to support their way of life. Famine and feast, the energy contained in the food supply, determines the size of a population. With the taming of plants and animals some twelve to fourteen thousand years ago, however, we exempted ourselves from this stern mandate. We hoisted ourselves our of our hunting-gathering niche, the only animals ever to break free of their biologically ordained profession. Now the last kind of large-scale hunting in which we still engage is that for seafood. We have allowed ourselves to stay put in one place, a way of life that led to social pathologies like bloody, knock-down, drag-out wars over disputed lands and resources; any war, for all that it may seem just, is more truly a counterproductive survival strategy, for the fittest are sent to kill and be killed while the least fit stay home to perpetuate the species. Another pathology is the creation of hierarchical, status-based communities, with a few kings and priests at the apex, a mort of pariahs and slaves at the nadir. Worst is the despoliation of habitat, the fouling of our own nests, that Paul Shepard deplores.

Eric Hoffer is right: we are unfinished. But will it matter if we never manage to finish ourselves? Upright humankind—as bipedal creatures, we suffer from flat feet, creaky knees, and crooked spines. The major discomfort, however, lies in our intrinsic Yahoodom and in the dislocations caused by clambering out of our preordained niche. There's no going back, of course. But there may be a remedy in firming up a vital part of our psychic anatomy, namely the backbone, which is another name for moral intelligence.

Firming up to finish ourselves might not be a bad thing. In search of a means, I ramble through the classical underbrush in my head—

Io driven flystung across the continent of Asia, the riddle of the Sphinx, and Proteus, the prophetic Old Man of the Sea, transforming himself from animal to flame to water to tree and back to god. I envision the modern incarnations of these myths—May's bloodthirsty deerflies, the sphinx moths with their horn-tailed larvae, and the dangerous shape-shifting dinoflagellates in coastal sounds and rivers. And I home in, as always, on the ancient Greek concept of *kairos*—balance, moderation—and on the classical certainty that, as Paul Shepard puts it, there is "livingness in the inanimate," that the world in all its manifestations is sentient and holy—from mountains, rivers, and constellations, from alpine flowers, minnows, and cottontails to biting flies and fish-killing protists. As long as we have no Proteus to prophesy the consequences of our actions, it's meet to remember that there is no stasis, that the balance always teeters. So, it is meet also that we behave ourselves and that we step with care between the vines—wherever they may be—and not on them.

Late March, and the Virginia Festival of the Book is under way— hundreds of programs at dozens of locations all over Charlottesville, Virginia. Downtown is a mob scene, with parking catch as catch can. I'm out in the boonies, however, at Ivy Creek Natural Area with two other writers who have been invited by The Nature Conservancy to discuss the importance of place in our work and lives. Rob Riordan, a black Irishman who is the Virginia chapter's director of communications, acts as moderator. One of my copanelists is Dick Austin, a Presbyterian minister, who preaches and writes about a theology-based environmentalism, then practices what he preaches on his homeplace farm in southwest Virginia; the other is Christopher Camuto, a hunter, hiker, and astute observer who has written eloquently about the attempt to restore red wolves to the Cherokee Mountains, as the Great Smokies were once called. More important, Chris tries not unsuccessfully to recover the Cherokees' perception of that rugged land as a place that is sentient and holy. I speak, of course, about my three countries, the mountain-walled Shenandoah Valley, the flat-as-a-flounder Carolina coast, and the invisible but equally real territory that is archaic Greece. Its principle of *kairos* is no less valid today than it was then. We talk, the three of us, about our passionate connections to specific places and about how caring for and respecting these places can inform our behavior toward the rest of the world. And every person in this room has this same splendid chance to let a particular attachment to one back yard, one town, one farm, one valley, one mountain range provide a model for the ways in which we might comport ourselves in regard to the greater whole.

The large community room in Ivy Creek's recreation building is nicely filled. I think, though, that the people who have come to hear us are among the converted—those, that is, who are well aware that humanity must somehow pull back lest we, like the snow geese, damage our living spaces beyond their ability to sustain us. The questions and comments flow readily. They are variously earnest, fearful, moralistic, and filled with silver-lining hope. As our time is almost up, Rob recognizes one last member of the audience. A middle-aged woman stands and says, "We really have to be careful. Mother Earth needs us."

I respond. "Careful, yes, but think about it. Earth needs us? Isn't it really the other way around?"

To arrive at a modus vivendi, to realize comfort at last, it might not be amiss to ask if *H. sapiens* is truly necessary We're not localized but pop up all over the globe. What good are Yahoos to the workings of the world? Of what possible use to eagle, shark, and flower-loving fly? What would fail and fall apart if an asteroid sent us the way of the dinosaurs or if we used our rightly prized technology to do ourselves in? It's quite safe to predict some effects of our withdrawal from the scene. There'd be fewer starlings, for lack of cleared land, and fewer brown-headed cowbirds, for lack of new edges and, thus, access to host nests where woods border building lots. Now-toxic, fish-killing dinoflagellates would be largely restored to primal quiescence because they would no longer be chemically overfed. The deepest South might well vanish beneath a virid smother of kudzu. And everywhere else, forests would regenerate, and fish stocks be replenished. But all life would still be subject to natural cycles of feast and famine, of increase and diminishment; all subject to natural forces that our kind has nothing to do with, like El Niño, typhoons and hurricanes, volcanic explosions, earthquakes, and planetwide warming or cooling (we do contribute to warming, but how much we contribute is a matter on which no definitive pronouncement has yet been made).

Our self-taught tendency toward despicability is not in doubt. We're also dispensable. Indeed, the world can do very well without us. It doesn't need us to keep it spinning around any more than it needs deer flies and screwworms, starlings, sandburs, and poison ivy.

Rather, it's we who need the world.

Yahoo

APPENDIX

House Mouse (*Mus musculus*)

The Despicables Ratings

What is your least favorite animal or plant? The one you despise most, the one you find totally useless, the one you'd love to see gone, and not just gone but gone forever?

That is the completely unscientific question that I've asked friends and strangers encountered in my peregrinations during the last few years. The list leans toward the Southern experience of despicable plants and creatures, for most of my time is spent in the American South. But answers have come from as far afield as Falmouth, Massachusetts; Hermosa, South Dakota; and Jerez, Mexico.

As anyone might have predicted, the living things most intensely disliked are those that impinge unpleasantly or painfully on human existence. They appear without warning. Some bite and sting, while others raise blisters. Some are invaders, crowding out native species. Some merely annoy, but others may kill. All of them, be they exotic or homegrown, are exceedingly abundant. Swat, spray, and smash as we will, there is no getting rid of them. And here's the list.

It begins with the hodgepodge of despicables that come in last, only one mention each—but look at their exuberant diversity. Each is identified here as closely as possible with its formal name; in many cases, however, it is the generic creature that is despised, and only a loose, general identification can be made. Comments in parentheses are those of sworn enemies.

molds, fungi of various families, genera, and species

anthrax bacterium, *Bacillus anthracis*

slime molds, protists

Giardia lamblia, a parasitic protozoan that causes severe intestinal
    distress
Pfiesteria piscicida, a dinoflagellate

bamboo, *Phyllostachys aureosulcata* and others, all of them ornamen-
    tal garden plants that tend to go invasively wild

beets, *Beta vulgaris* ("I dislike their texture, their taste, their smell.")

common chickweed, *Stellaria media* ("It doesn't know when to stop.")

Eurasian milfoil, *Myriophyllum* spp., imported takeover water plants

ferns, order Filicales ("plants without character invariably used in restaurants without character")

greenbriar, *Smilax* spp.

Japanese honeysuckle, *Lonicera japonica* ("a curse on all")

jimsonweed, *Datura stramonium* ("offending prickers")

melaleuca, *Melaleuca quinquenervia*, an Australian tree that has become a pest species in Florida

nut grass, *Cyperus esculentus*

pennywort, *Hydrocotyle bonariensis*

phragmites, *Phragmites communis*, a nonnative wetlands plant, the presence of which indicates environmental degradation

pines, *Pinus* spp., any and all of them

rabbit tobacco, *Gnaphalium obtusifolium*

red-hot poker, *Kniphofia* spp. ("Summer is hot enough without having to look at those blazing spires. And the color does not blend well with *any* other color.")

Russian thistle, *Salsola kali* var. *tenuifolia*, an accidentally introduced Russian plant that is not a thistle but rather a member of the goosefoot family

salt-cedar, also known as tamarisk, *Tamarix chinensis*, an invasive exotic of the West

wire grass, also called Bermuda grass, *Cynodon dactylon* ("the plant that fights back unfairly")

yucca, *Yucca filamentosa* ("Those leaves remind me of swords and the stringy bits, of spider webs.")

ants in general, family Formicidae

earwigs, order Dermaptera, many families

louse, both *Pediculus humanus*, the head louse, and *Phthirus pubis*, the pubic louse termites, order Isoptera, many families

wasps and hornets, order Hymenoptera, many families

scorpions, Arachnida, order Scorpionida

zebra mussel, *Dreissena polymorpha*

sharks, class Chondrichthyes, many families

American eel, *Anguilla rostrata*

cat, *Felis catus*

chipmunk, *Tamias* spp.

coyote, *Canis latrans* ("They killed my cats!")

hyena, family Hyaenidae ("I've never seen one, but something about their looks and their scavenger lifestyle is tremendously unpleasant.")

mole, *Scalopus aquaticus*

opossum, *Didelphis marsupialis*

woodchuck, also known as groundhog, *Marmota monax*

Some of these votes may have been influenced by the environmental press. Two of the one-vote despicables, for example, appear on The Nature Conservancy's "dirty dozen" list of the least wanted species in America, and two others from that list show up later in my ratings. According to *Nature Conservancy* magazine (November-December 1996), the least wanted include the freshwater zebra mussel and the salt-cedar tree, each one an introduced species and both mentioned on my list above. Two others, which pulled in more than a single vote from my respondents, figure below: the purple loosestrife plant and the brown tree snake. Others of The Nature Conservancy's dirty dozen are the plants hydrilla, *Hydrilla verticillata;* leafy spurge, *Euphorbia esula;* miconia, *Miconia calvescens;* and Chinese tallow, *Sapium sebiferum.* One insect shows up, the balsam woolly adelgid, *Adelges piceae,* which attacks hemlocks; one terrestrial mollusk, the rosy wolfsnail, *Euglandina rosea;* and two marine species, the flathead catfish, *Pylodictis olivaris,* and the green crab, *Carcinus maenas.*

In my survey, the living things rating two votes each are: cocklebur, *Xanthium pensylvanicum;* crabgrass, *Digitaria sanguinalis* ("almost malignant"); tapeworm, class Cestoda; leech, class Hirudinea; house centipede, *Scutigera coleoptrata;* crickets in the house, subfamily Grylli-nae (the qualifier "in the house" was specified both times); rock dove, *Columba livia* ("rats with wings"); starling, *Sturnus vulgaris;* bats, order Chiroptera; and *Homo sapiens.*

The following life-forms received three votes each: purple loosestrife, *Lythrum salicaria,* an aggressive imported plant; slugs, order Stylommatophora; sea nettle jellyfish, *Chrysaora quinquecirrha;* rodentkind, specifically mice, rats, and squirrels, *Mus, Rattus,* and *Sci-urus* spp. respectively; and viruses, with special mention going to those for AIDS and the common cold. Of the rat, one sworn enemy writes, "No matter how rural and wholesome its habitat, it always looks *sordid,* as if it had come out of a sewer. The bristles on its oth-erwise naked tail are almost supernaturally repulsive."

Pulling in considerably more votes, with each earning about a third of the total earned by the most despicable species on the list, are two insects, fire ants, *Solenopsis* spp., and fleas, order Siphon-aptera; and one grass, the sandbur, sometimes called sandspur, *Cenchrus* spp.

Second place is clogged by scourges that have individually racked up close to half the votes awarded to the winners of the despicable ratings. The occupants of the second-place niche are another insect, cockroaches, order Blattodea, family Blattidae; three kinds of arachnid—ticks, chiggers, and spiders; snakes; and one plant—you guessed it—poison ivy, *Rhus radicans.* With spiders, the generic kind figures most often in the tally, but several people par-ticularly nominated the brown recluse, *Loxosceles reclusa,* and the black widow, *Latrodectus mactans.* Snakes, too, are mainly a generic category; to many of us, a snake is a snake is a snake, and has been so ever since Eden. One person, however, appended the word "poi-sonous," while a few people were definite, naming rattlesnake, *Cro-talus* and *Sistrurus* spp.; copperhead, *Agkistrodon contortrix;* cotton-mouth moccasin, *A. piscivorus;* and brown tree snake, *Boigo irregularis.*

(The last is a Far Eastern species introduced to islands in the Pacific; it has caused notable devastation to Guam's native wildlife, and there are fears that it may have reached Hawaii.)

And the worst of all, the greatest villains, the nastiest, the most despised? No contest here: the Diptera, the two-winged flies, swarm far ahead of the rest of the pack. They are despised by twice as many people as any other plant or creature on my list. Just plain flies, without any further qualification, were mentioned more often than not, but specific kinds were also damned: fruit flies, *Drosophila* spp.; houseflies, *Musca domestica;* deerflies, *Chrysops* spp.; the rabbit botfly, *Cuterebra cuniculi;* mosquitoes, family Culicidae; true gnats, members of several Dipteran families (which suffer from a bad press but are generally harmless); and no-see-ums, members of the family Ceratopogonidae (which most emphatically are not). The last have been characterized by one hapless victim as "jaws with wings."

Here the list ends, though any number of other species might be added. It will quickly be noted that some of the plants and creatures, like kudzu and hornworms, that I have written about make no appearance whatsoever on the list above, but they earn their own stories because of this conviction: they are so ubiquitous and so insufferably part of our lives that someone would have nominated them eventually. It will also be noted that the stories in this book do not include some of our most egregiously awful animal and vegetable pests. Some of the omissions in this book are due simply to the dizzying difficulties of having to focus on a particular one or two species out of the thousands possible, as with mosquitoes (though I could have chosen a monstrously large model with black-striped legs, the gallinipper, more formally known as *Psorophora ciliata,* which rises with a lusty and well-nigh unquenchable thirst during Great Neck Point's wetter summers.) Other omissions have received full discussion in other publications. Poison ivy, slugs, and cockroaches, for example, have been exhaustively examined in recent books, each scrupulously informed but nonacademic, and each devoted obsessively to the particular despicable species. I myself have treated elsewhere of such things as ticks and chiggers, jellyfish and snakes. But for anyone whose curiosity is still unslaked, an unapologetically selective booklist is included after the Notes section to help appease any lingering fancy for further investigation.

NOTES

Full citations appear in the bibliography.

page xi   epigraph: Fabre, *The Passionate Observer*, 91.

Living Together, Like It or Not

10   "are not only cold-blooded": Dillard, *Pilgrim at Tinker Creek*, 64.

10   "No monkey makes light of shapes": Shepard, *The Tender Carnivore and the Sacred Game*, 47.

11   "embedded in our genetic memory": Conniff, *Spineless Wonders*, 108.

13   "What is not useful": Mather quoted by Matthiessen, *Wildlife in America*, 57.

14   "Swatting a mosquito": Evans, *The Pleasures of Entomology*, 11.

14   "if we are justified": Hubbell, *Broadsides from the Other Orders*, 85.

15   "What problems and characteristics": Shepard, 41.

Prospect and Refuge: Sandburs

23   "Spikelets 1-flowered": *Gray's New Manual of Botany*, 119.

23   "Unpleasant": Kraus, *A Guide to Ocean Dune Plants*, 59.

23   "Horribly spiny flower clusters": Brown, *Grasses*, 99.

24   It has been noted: Martin, *Weeds*, 27.

The Barkings of a Joyful Squirrel: Gray Squirrel

30   "He has not Wings": Lawson, *A New Voyage to Carolina*, 130.

32   "to a local officer": Kalm, *Travels in North America*, 52.

32   "Squirrels are the chief food": Kalm, 52.

33   "when the corn is juicy": Audubon, *Journals*, Vol. II, 496.

33   "the barkings of a joyful Squirrel": Audubon, *Journals*, 404.

33   *"Barking off Squirrels"*: Audubon, *Journals*, 460.

Murmurations: European Starling

48   ". . . said he would not ransom Mortimer": Shakespeare, *King Henry IV, Part I*, I.iii.219–26.

53 "That was lovely": Mozart quoted by Biancolli, *The Mozart Handbook*, 396.

53 "Full of wrong notes": Biancolli, 511.

53 "The Starlings are found": Cassell, *Natural History*, quoted in the *Oxford English Dictionary*.

61 "As if out of the Bible": Updike, "The Great Scarf of Birds," *Collected Poems*, 37–38.

62 "Since we never consider as a nuisance": Corbo, *Arnie, the Darling Starling*, 79.

The Natural History of Proteus: Pfiesteria piscicida

67 "immortal Old Man": Homer, *The Odyssey*, Fagles translation, 4.431.

67 "swarming sea": Homer, 4.436, 4.477; other places.

67 "muster your heart": Homer, 4.466–71.

75 Yet a third element in fish killer's transformation: Shoemaker, "Fish Kills, Facts, and Pfiesteria."

A Foot in the Door: The Fungi

91 "This is the foul fiend": Shakespeare, *King Lear*, III.iv.118.

92 One notable mycologist: Schaecter, *In the Company of Mushrooms*, 34.

93 *"Our kind multiplies"*: Plath, *Collected Poems*, 140.

The Creature with Nineteen Lives: Common Opossum

98 "An Opassum hath a head": Captain John Smith, *A map of Virginia with a description of the country*, 1612, quoted in the *Oxford English Dictionary*.

98 "The Weather was very cold": Lawson, *A New Voyage to Carolina*, 31.

98 "The *Possum* is found": Lawson, 125–26.

Legs: Centipedes

118 "The centipede was happy quite": Mrs. Edward Craster, 1871, from *Bartlett's Familiar Quotations*, 13th ed., 750.

120 So it is reasonably thought . . . they had to find food: Manton, *Arthropoda*, 283–85.

122 "stumble on food by accident": Manton, 395.

122 One large scolopendrid: Manton, 391.

126 "by a series of gaits": Manton, 282.

Heritage: Kudzu

136 "an awful tangled nuisance": Fairchild quoted by Shurtleff and Aoyagi, *The Book of Kudzu*, 12.

143 "Japan invades": Dickey, *Helmets*, 38.

The Wisdom of Nature: Brown-Headed Cowbird

156 "The bird is entirely brown": Catesby quoted in Feduccia, *Catesby's Birds of Colonial America*, 124.

158 "If we are fond"; "This is a mystery": Audubon, *Original Water-Color Paintings*, Plate 59.

160 Orians has asked five questions: Orians, *Blackbirds of the Americas*, 77.

160 "This suggests": Orians, 79.

163 Why did brood parasitism evolve: Orians, 87.

The Dew Lovers: Drosophila Fruit Flies

169 "The little fruit flies": Linsenmaier, *Insects of the World*, 258.

170 "as a swarm of flies": Milton, *Paradise Regained*, IV.15–17.

177 "1. Intense nearly continuous grooming": McClung and Hirsh, "Stereotypic behavioral responses to free-base cocaine and the development of behavioral sensitization in *Drosophila*," 109.

178 "Human counterparts": Greenspan, "Understanding the Genetic Construction of Behavior," 78.

Unfinished Business: Homo sapiens

182 epigraph: Hoffer, *Between the Devil and the Dragon*, 14.

183 "I never beheld": Swift, *Gulliver's Travels*, 215.

184 "the most unteachable of all animals": Swift, 251.

184   "begging, robbing, stealing": Swift, 239.

184   "my family, my friends": Swift, 261–62.

186   "has to finish himself": Hoffer, 22.

186   "more than just a physical place": Colinvaux, *Why Big Fierce Animals Are Rare*, 11.

188   "At last count": Weidensaul, *Living on the Wind*, 223.

191   "Large human populations": Shepard, *The Tender Carnivore*, 104.

191   "Environmental requirements are greater": Shepard, 121.

191   And humankind . . . "deeper into the scene": Falk, Kaplan, and Kaplan quoted in Hiss, *The Experience of Place*, 36–41.

193   "livingness in the inanimate": Shepard, 167.

FOR THE BOOKWORM

A Reading Guide

DESPICABLES ONE AT A TIME

Adler, Bill, Jr. *Outwitting Squirrels: 101 Cunning Stratagems to Reduce Dramatically the Egregious Misappropriation of Seed from Your Birdfeeder by Squirrels.* Chicago: Chicago Review Press, 1988.

    A compendium of maneuvers, some clever, some downright silly, to foil the furry marauders. Failure is assured.

Anderson, Thomas E. *The Poison Ivy, Oak and Sumac Book: A Short Natural History and Cautionary Account.* Ukiah, California: Acton Circle, 1995.

    A lively guide to *Toxicodendron*, the "poison-tree," including sections on how its oils affect humankind (a fulminating allergic reaction), how to cope with the allergy—and the plants themselves, and how to enter the annual Poison Oak Show held as part of a fall festival in Columbia, California. Many illustrations, from reproductions of old botanical prints to range maps and color photographs.

Cabe, Paul R. *European Starling,* No. 48 in The Birds of North America. Philadelphia: The Academy of Natural Sciences; Washington, D.C.: American Ornithologists' Union, 1993.

    Twenty-four pages that lucidly present the scientific facts about the bird and its rampage through the New World.

Gordon, David George. *The Compleat Cockroach.* Berkeley, California: Ten Speed Press, 1996.

_____. *Field Guide to the Slug.* Western Society of Malacologists. Seattle: Sasquatch Books, 1994.

    Short books both, with ample illustrations that help much to distinguish the German cockroach from, say, the wood cockroach and the banana slug from all others, large and small.

Hauser, Susan Carol. *Nature's Revenge: The Secrets of Poison Ivy, Poison Oak, Poison Sumac, and Their Remedies.* New York: Lyons & Burford, 1996.

    A slender volume that focuses on urushiol, the plants' toxic oil, and the "dastardly itching" that it almost inevitably causes. Learn here how it's possible to contract a raging case of poison ivy without even getting near the stuff. Learn, too, the soothing secrets of rubbing alcohol, hot water, and corticosteroids.

Hilyard, Paul. *The Book of the Spider: From Arachnophobia to the Love of Spiders.* New York: Random House, 1994.

    From page 80: "When Professor John Henry Comstock of Cornell

University was asked by a visitor, 'What good are spiders?' he replied, 'What good are they? They are damned interesting.'" Spider flight, spider silk-making, spider venom, spider myths, and much else are explained here in easily readable terms by a true arachnophile.

Lehane, Brendan. *The Compleat Flea*. New York: The Viking Press, 1969.
    A circus of flea facts and lore, from physiology and curious adaptations to specific hosts to the creature's role as muse to both Mussorgsky and sundry pornographers.

Shurtleff, William, and Akiko Aoyagi. *The Book of Kudzu: A Culinary and Healing Guide*. Wayne, New Jersey: Avery Publishing Group, Inc., 1985.
    A slim, elegantly illustrated volume on the botany, history, and human uses of the vine, along with a grand soup-to-cough-syrup compendium of recipes.

ECLECTIC COLLECTIONS

Berenbaum, May. *Ninety-nine Gnats, Nits, and Nibblers*. Urbana and Chicago: University of Illinois Press, 1989.

_____. *Ninety-nine More Maggots, Mites, and Munchers*. Urbana and Chicago: University of Illinois Press, 1993.
    True tales about a wriggle of bugs, a writhing of worms, a loop of caterpillars, and a buzzing of flies. But sublimities like luna moths and fireflies are included, along with a multitude of small horrors like tent caterpillars, bagworms, bed bugs, and chicken lice.

Colinvaux, Paul. *Why Big Fierce Animals Are Rare: An Ecologist's Perspective*. Princeton, New Jersey: 1978.
    Answers to questions like, Why are there so many species of living things and why far more of some than others? Chapters include "Why the Sea Is Blue," "The Nation States of Trees," "The Social Lives of Plants," and, not least, "The People's Place."

Conniff, Richard. *Spineless Wonders: Strange Tales from the Invertebrate World*. New York: Henry Holt and Company, Inc., 1996.
    Visits with creatures, here held safely captive in print, that often inspire fear or loathing. One is monstrously larger than man, the others far smaller: giant squid, flies, leeches, fire ants, dragonflies,

tarantulas, fleas, ground beetles, earthworms, mosquitoes, moths, and hagfish, also known as slime eels. The essays entertain as they inform. Conniff has done the same thing for animals with backbones—sharks, moles, bats, bloodhounds "in full slobber," and many others—in *Every Creeping Thing: True Tales of Faintly Repulsive Wildlife*, Holt, 1998.

Lembke, Janet. *Looking for Eagles: Reflections of a Classical Naturalist.* Lyons & Burford, 1990.

Essays on earthbound creatures encountered while keeping eyes on the sky. Among those that may be considered irredeemably horrid are ticks, snakes, toads, jellyfish, and a parasitic isopod.

THE HUMAN CONDITION

Hoffer, Eric. "On Nature and Human Nature," in the anthology *Between the Devil and the Dragon.* New York: Harper & Row, Publishers, 1982.

The views of an insightful and unregenerate curmudgeon, who writes with the passion of true belief. From page 37 "Man's being an unfinished, defective animal has been the root of his uniqueness and creativeness. He is the only animal not satisfied with being what he is."

Matthiessen, Peter. *Wildlife in America.* New York: The Viking Press, 1959.

A detailed account of the ways in which human alteration of the land—through activities like farming, logging, and hunting—have affected indigenous North American plants and animals since the days of European exploration and colonization. Citing observers from Captain John Smith and Cotton Mather to John Muir and more contemporary naturalists, Matthiessen makes extensive use of the historical record to document the changes.

Shepard, Paul. *The Tender Carnivore and the Sacred Game.* Athens and London: The University of Georgia Press, 1998. Originally published by Scribner in 1973.

An examination of human ecology, from our emergence as hunter-gatherers, with bodies specifically evolved to fit this niche, to our abandonment of the niche and the subsequent disjuncture between what we were biologically designed to do and what we have invented for ourselves to do, like binding ourselves to farms and cities. Shepard explains our evolution both physiologically and spiritually, with keen attention to the natural world around us as the means by which we form a compact with and a necessary reverence for other life. But even at this late date, and in these parlous times, he holds out hope that humankind may reconnect, in ways appropriate to this era of technology, with our true role.

GENERAL BIBLIOGRAPHY

Audubon, John James. *The Original Water-Color Paintings for* The Birds of America. New York: American Heritage Publishing Co., Inc., 1966.

Audubon, Marie R. *Audubon and His Journals.* Vol. I. New York: Dover Publications, Inc., 1994.

_____. *Audubon and His Journals.* Vol. II. New York: Dover Publications, Inc., 1986.

Biancolli, Lewis, ed. *The Mozart Handbook.* Cleveland and New York: The World Publishing Company, 1954.

Borror, Donald, and Richard E. White. *A Field Guide to the Insects of America North of Mexico.* The Peterson Field Guide Series. Boston: Houghton Mifflin Company, 1970.

Brown, Lauren. *Grasses: An Identification Guide.* Boston: Houghton Mifflin Company, 1979.

Burkholder, JoAnn M., and Howard B. Glasgow, Jr. "Interactions of a Toxic Estuarine Dinoflagellate with Microbial Predators and Prey," *Archiv für Protisten Kunde,* Vol. 145 (1995), pp. 177–88.

Burkholder, JoAnn M., Howard B. Glasgow, Jr., and Cecil W. Hobbs. "Fish Kills Linked to a Toxic Ambush-Predator Dinoflagellate: Distribution and Environmental Conditions," *Marine Ecology Progress Series,* Vol. 124 (1995), pp. 43–61.

Burt, William Henry, and Richard Philip Grossenheider. *A Field Guide to the Mammals.* Boston: Houghton Mifflin Company, 1961.

Christensen, Clyde M. *The Molds and Man: An Introduction to the Fungi.* 2nd ed. Minneapolis: University of Minnesota Press, 1961.

Corbo, Margarete Sigl, and Diane Marie Barras. *Arnie, the Darling Starling.* Boston: Houghton Mifflin Company, 1983.

Covell, Charles V., Jr. *A Field Guide to the Moths: Eastern North America.* The Peterson Field Guide Series. Boston: Houghton Mifflin Company, 1984.

Dickey, James. *Helmets.* Middletown, Connecticut: Wesleyan University Press, 1964.

Dillard, Annie. *Pilgrim at Tinker Creek.* New York: Harper & Row, Publishers, Inc., 1974.

Evans, Howard Ensign. *The Pleasures of Entomology: Portraits of Insects and the People Who Study Them.* Washington, D.C.: Smithsonian Institution Press, 1985.

Everest, John W., James H. Miller, Donald M. Ball, and Michael G. Patterson. "Kudzu in Alabama." Alabama Cooperative Extension Service, Auburn University, Alabama. Circular ANR-65.

Fabre, Jean Henri. *The Passionate Observer: Writings from the World of Nature.* San Francisco: Chronicle Books, 1998.

Feare, Christopher. *The Starling.* Oxford and New York: Oxford University Press, 1984.

Feduccia, Alan, ed. *Catesby's Birds of Colonial America.* Chapel Hill and London: The University of North Carolina Press, 1985.

Fichter, George S. *Insect Pests.* New York: Golden Press, 1966.

Gray's New Manual of Botany: A Handbook of the Flowering Plants and Trees of the Central and Northeastern United States and Adjacent Canada. Rearranged and revised by Benjamin Lincoln Robinson and Merritt Lyndon Fernald. New York: American Book Company, 1908.

Greenspan, Ralph J. "Understanding the Genetic Construction of Behavior." *Scientific American,* No. 272 (April 1995), pp. 72–78.

Hiss, Tony. *The Experience of Place.* New York: Alfred A. Knopf, 1990.

Homer. *The Odyssey.* Robert Fagles, trans. New York: Viking Penguin, 1996.

Hoots, Diane, and Juanitta Baldwin. *Kudzu; The Vine to Love or Hate.* Kodak, Tennessee: Suntop Press, 1996.

Hubbell, Sue. *Broadsides from the Other Orders: A Book of Bugs.* New York: Random House, 1993.

Kalm, Peter. *Travels in North America: The English Version of 1770.* New York: Dover Publications, Inc., 1964.

Kraus, E. Jean Wilson. *A Guide to Ocean Dune Plants Common to North Carolina.* Chapel Hill: The University of North Carolina Press, 1988.

Lawson, John. *A New Voyage to Carolina.* Hugh Talmage Lefler, ed. Chapel Hill: The University of North Carolina Press, 1967.

Leahy, Christopher. *The Birdwatcher's Companion; An Encyclopedic Handbook of North American Birdlife.* New York: Bonanza Books, 1952.

Levi, Herbert W., and Lorna R. Levi. *A Guide to Spiders and Their Kin.* New York: Golden Press, 1968.

Lincoff, Gary H. *The Audubon Society Field Guide to North American Mushrooms.* New York: Alfred A. Knopf, 1981.

Linsenmaier, Walter. *Insects of the World.* Translated from the German by Leigh E. Chadwick. New York: McGraw-Hill Book Company, 1972.

Manton, S. M. *The Arthropoda: Habits, Functional Morphology, and Evolution.* Oxford: Clarendon Press, 1977.

Martin, Alexander. *Weeds.* Racine, Wisconsin: Western Publishing Company, Inc., 1972.

McClung, Colleen, and Jay Hirsh. "Stereotypic behavioral responses to free-base cocaine and the development of behavioral sensitization in *Drosophila.*" *Current Biology,* Vol. 8, No. 2 (15 January 1998), pp. 109–12.

Milne, Lorus, and Margery Milne. *National Audubon Society Field Guide to North American Insects and Spiders.* New York: Alfred A. Knopf, 1980.

Orians, Gordon. *Blackbirds of the Americas.* Seattle and London: University of Washington Press, 1985.

Plath, Sylvia. *The Collected Poems.* Ted Hughes, ed. New York: Harper & Row, Publishers, 1981.

Schaecter, Elio. *In the Company of Mushrooms: A Biologist's Tale.* Cambridge, Massachusetts: Harvard University Press, 1997.

Shoemaker, Ritchie C. "Fish Kills, Facts and Pfiesteria: My Patients and the River Told Me What I Had to Know." *The Washington Post,* September 21, 1997, p. c1.

Stokes, Donald. *A Guide to Observing Insect Lives*. Boston: Little, Brown and Company, 1983.

Swift, Jonathan. *Gulliver's Travels and Other Writings*. New York: Bantam Books, 1962.

Updike, John. *Collected Poems, 1953–1993*. New York: Alfred A. Knopf, 1995.

Waldbauer, Gilbert. *The Birder's Bug Book*. Cambridge, Massachusetts: Harvard University Press, 1998.

Webster, William David, James E. Parnell, and Walter C. Biggs, Jr. *Mammals of the Carolinas, Virginia, and Maryland*. Chapel Hill and London: The University of North Carolina Press, 1985.

Weidensaul, Scott. *Living on the Wind: Across the Globe with Migratory Birds*. New York: North Point Press, 1999.

Wilson, Edward O. *The Insect Societies*. Cambridge, Massachusetts: Harvard University Press, 1971.

Zim, Herbert S., and Robert T. Mitchell. *Butterflies and Moths*. New York: Golden Press, Inc., 1964.